TRIPE 'n' TROTTERS

'Tales of a Post-War Northern Childhood'

by

Brian Carline

Illustrated by David Summerville

**Grosvenor House
Publishing Limited**

This book is published by
Grosvenor House Publishing Ltd
28-30 High Street, Guildford, Surrey, GU1 3EL.
www.grosvenorhousepublishing.co.uk

A CIP record for this book
is available from the British Library

ISBN 978-1-908596-99-4

Dedication

For Monica, Charlotte, Lucy,
Christopher and Helen

CONTENTS

Preface

The late forties and early fifties was an era of recovery and an awakening from the misery and hardship of the Second World War. Salford, a typical northern industrial city, was, and still is, an impoverished area with its associated problems of indigence and lack of optimism. Its poor housing engendered feelings of hopelessness and desperation from its residents. Nevertheless, the rent man still called at these premises with a purposeful knock that would wake the dead. This landscape of identical grimy streets, many with their corner shop and pub, presented an uninspiring and austere panorama. A cold, damp climate brought with it chronic bronchitis, whilst malnutrition and sullied living conditions nurtured disease, and a higher than average infant mortality.

It was the age when children were tempted by new and exciting purchases in shop windows. Uncle Joe's Mintballs nestled alongside Spangles, Barrett's sweet cigarettes and penny chews. Newsagents sold The Dandy, Eagle, Bunty and Judy. The adults saw the advent of the term 'hire purchase' giving an air of respectability to paying for things on the drip. The radio gave us programmes that would draw huge audiences. The tinkling sounds of: 'Have A Go Joe' and the iconic Wilfred Pickles cheered factory workforces, often giving its employees hope for a new three-piece suite when they heard the words, 'Give him the money, Mabel'.

Salford folk, in common with residents of any post-war industrial city, have always shown resilience and an ability to bounce back in adversity. Above all, they have an irrepressible sense of humour despite their misfortunes. I recall a trader on Salford market whose *nom de plume* was Barmy Mick, so-called because his stock was sold at such low prices. A punter returned to his stall to complain that the electric toaster she'd recently purchased from him, worked on some days but not on others. She asked of him,

'I know it's got "variable toaster" on its box, Mick, but my God, does that mean heat or the days it works?'

Nobody had central heating or fitted carpets. Linoleum was cold to the feet and made you jump into bed quickly. The majority had to endure outside toilets and the 'Jerry' under the bed. Washtubs with cushions in the bottom doubled as play pens for infants. Only a select few had television and the monochrome picture on its microscopic screen was only possible if you juggled the aerial. Consequently Rin Tin Tin could take on a rabid appearance as its speckled image bounced up and down.

Flatley washing machines vibrated their way across your kitchen floor. Savage mangles removed water from clothes, and fingers from hands if you weren't too careful. Milk went 'off' quickly in the warmer months. Dog poo was often white in colour. Large families had to bed their children 'top and tail' with three to a bed, and you were extremely unlucky if the other two were bed-wetters.

'Which end do you want tonight, Eddie?' a mother would ask one of her sons.

'The shallow end, mum,' came his desperate response.

Kids' clothing frequently operated on the bequeathal principle, and the youngest members of the family wore shirts and pullovers two sizes too big for them. Shoes could be stuffed with newspaper to prevent feet slipping around inside, and in extremely impecunious times the tips would be cut off plimsolls to get an extra few weeks' mileage out of them. Mittens would be connected to winter coats by a line of wool running from one sleeve to the other, whilst balaclavas made us all look like paediatric members of the SAS.

There was nothing better at giving you energy than a sugar butty. Bread and dripping gave you warmth, vitality and a permanent fatty film inside your mouth. Its taste was wonderful and deserved a Michelin star. Fish and chip shops fried their wares in beef lard, producing a taste both your tongue and arteries would never forget. Yorkshire pudding was served up for Sunday dinner in a huge tray. Soak this in gravy made from meat fat, vegetable water, gravy browning and cornflower, and you had a food that would make Greek Gods reject Ambrosia. The practice was to consume this filling starter before the main meal – that's because there wasn't much of the main meal.

Cod liver oil was the panacea for warding off all kinds of ailments and Andrews Liver Salts purged many a gall bladder. Every family possessed a tooth comb. Boils were a common side-effect of poor health and were remedied by a bread poultice or lanced by a physician (or a grandma if it was a weekend). Visits to the dentist were feared because of crude anaesthesia, pain and the prospect of wearing ill-fitting National Health dentures. Chiropodists witnessed malformed feet due to incorrect sized foot-wear. Hospital wards were as long as the *Champs Elysees* and doctors wore stethoscopes made from rubber Bunsen burner tubing.

If the 1950s was a part of your childhood and you would like to revisit these formative years, then this collection of stories will remind you of much of the above. If your memory lane had cobbled streets void of cars, houses with freshly 'stoned' doorsteps and a bombsite characteristically swathed in pink, rose bay willow herb. If your mates were boys wearing Davy Crockett hats and girls with ribbons in their hair playing on roller skates, then please read on and take with you in this journey your sense of humour.

The cryptic title, 'Tripe and Trotters', stems from one of the stories in this anthology.

Brian Carline, July 2011

Our Ged

Sandwiched between the grimy Brunswick Methodist Church, Dr Goldstein's surgery and the Pendleton Tabernacle was Strawberry Road. As with the majority of other cobbled Salford streets, all of the terraced two-up, two-downs looked identical with the exception of 'The Hooleys'. They were an Irish family of nine whose property still bore the effects of Hitler's wrath. A land mine, jettisoned by a myopic German bomb aimer eight years earlier, had failed to incapacitate Salford docks, instead, levelling the Co-op funeral parlour, the Central cinema and taking away the chimney stack and end wall of the Hooley residence. Such a readjustment in its masonry had remained untouched since then.

The principal road through Salford was Broad Street and this acted as a boundary line between three distinct demographic groups in the area. To the north was Eccles Old Road, with its chichi middle class ensconced in semi-detached houses. Their occupants were the 'Haves' of the city. To the east was us in Strawberry Road, the 'Have-Nots', and to the west, Hanky Park, the 'Have-Absolutely-Bugger-Alls'. We in the east rather misguidedly believed we were a cut above this lot. The cut, if any, was microscopic. Hanky Park bore its name from Hankinson Street, the main artery of this impoverished and deprived part of the parish. The street fed row after row of drab back-to-back terraced houses, inhabited by poverty-stricken families whose only optimism was a few shillings' win on the 3.15 at Haydock or a few pints on a Saturday night. The squalid and overcrowded buildings were said to breed strength of character and a resoluteness of the people who lived there. All I saw was a breeding ground for polio and tuberculosis.

There was a sense of rivalry between the kids from the latter two districts and such antagonism would spawn gangs. A typical gang would include youngsters of a broad spectrum of ages. The senior members would usually be the fourteen-year-olds and, during their sorties into enemy territory, they would be accompanied by fellow acolytes some as young as five or six. These callow members would wave sticks and push out their tongues as a form of aggression. The band of reprobates was usually of mixed gender. Indeed, some of the best fighters were girls.

Our gang was really no different in structure and its leader was Frankie Beardall. Frank was the obvious choice for supremo. He could do such amazing things. He reminded us of Humphrey Bogart because of his ability to blow beautifully formed smoke rings. Such savoir faire gave him tremendous kudos, allowing him to tutor his motley companions in how to smoke. His fearless stunts would make your heart race. The most famous example being his leap from Cock Robin Bridge onto the carriage roof of a Blackpool-bound train.

Our disparate bunch was usually ten in number, except on a Friday when Irene Wilkinson and her brother Alec had to visit the local health clinic for their sun ray treatment, dose of cod liver oil and malt extract. Alec suffered from rickets and was a hopeless goalkeeper.

One of the Hanky Park gangs was the Rossall Street firm. Their reputation was that of a malevolent crew who would sell their own grannies for a few Woodbines. If something was not cemented in or screwed down on a Salford street, it immediately became the property of the Rossall Street gang.

My childhood memories of Salford are in monochrome. These recollections are of the days before 'The Clean Air Act'. Continuous wreaths of smoke from nearby Trafford Park hung defiantly in the air, occluding much of the sunlight. The air you breathed was a curious mixture of the smell of roasted cornflakes from the Kellogg's factory and the burnt hydrocarbons donated by Greengate and Irwell rubber works. It was on one of these grey, yet surprisingly warm summer days that we were visited by Lezzo.

Lezzo (Leslie Walter Batty), was commander in chief of the Rossall Street mob and a most objectionable adolescent. I suppose in medical terms he would be described as pathologically unsuitable to society and would soon cause the Manchester and Salford Crime Squad problems for years to come. His intimidating presence at the top of our street precipitated panic and alarm amongst us. Such misgivings caused the horrified Herbie Donnelly to uncontrollably wet himself at the sight of the villain. Herbie was a sickly boy, who always wore lop-sided national health spectacles and a leather helmet to keep them in place.

The Australian cricket team were touring the country and currently playing at Lancashire's ground, Old Trafford. The city's youth was cricket crazy. Lezzo was here on our turf to challenge us to a cricket match. Frankie bravely swaggered up our street to meet the menacing teenager.

Lezzo's sentences were usually peppered with expletives, coupled with repetitive bouts of spitting. Indeed, he used words that even Herbie's dad wouldn't use and he could swear. We heard him give Mr Serafini, the ice cream man, a mouthful when his horse deposited most of the contents of its lower bowel, outside the Donnelly's front door.

'We'll be England and you lot 'll be them Aussie buggers!' proclaimed Lezzo. 'We'll play yer on t' cinders by t'side o' t' Bridge,' he eloquently explained. The Bridge was a pub that had remarkably survived the bombs years earlier. Sadly, the adjacent property, ironically named Tanner's Leather Works, had not and its shattered remains had been levelled and covered with cinders. The cinder croft, as we all called it, was our principal recreation site for football, cricket, bogey racing (a small cart with pram wheels), hop-scotch and allies (marbles).

'Ave any of you gorra bat, cos we'll have to use it as well?' Lezzo enquired.

'No chance, Lezzo!' snapped Frankie. 'Get yer own bat. Last time we played you at footy, you nicked our casey (a leather football).'

Now I thought that was remarkably brave of Frankie. Lezzo was like sweating gelignite and could explode for no reason. However, Lezzo seemed surprisingly unaffected by Frankie's aggressive riposte.

'Just gerra team and we'll smash the arse off ya. We'll be over tomorra mornin',' he threatened.

The sight of Lezzo crossing Broad Street and returning to his enclave was a sense of relief for us all, particularly Herbie who was now completely drenched from the waist down. Frankie returned from his unnerving encounter and gathered us around him. It was time to discuss serious tactics.

Charlie Sago would open the batting, after all, it was his bat. I have to say it was a pretty impressive team. Alec wanted to be wicket keeper but was quickly dissuaded from undertaking this role for anatomical reasons. He was substituted by his sister, Irene. She was a safer pair of hands with no immediate signs of bowed legs.

Our secret weapon was my brother, Ged. Ged had suffered from cerebral palsy from birth. His disability meant he was partially paralysed down the left side of his body and often needed a wheelchair to get around. In those days the term cerebral palsy was not in use, instead victims of this disability were ungraciously referred to as 'spastics'.

Ged's lack of mobility on his left side was compensated for by his right, his right arm was strong and powerfully toned. Arm wrestling was his speciality and kids would queue up at parties to take him on. They would bet their party bags they could overpower him, but Ged would return home laden with sherbet fizzes, penny spanish, love hearts and plastic novelties as his spoils of war.

Ged would open the bowling. We had found that if one of us pushed his wheelchair at speed along his run up to the wicket, Ged could release the ball from his right arm with tremendous speed. His bowling repertoire included swingers and beamers of such velocity he was the 'Fiery Fred' of Strawberry Road.

Irene's dad had kindly cut up pieces of a wooden beer crate on which he painted white stumps and bails. A house brick placed behind it would prevent it from falling over, except when struck by the cricket ball. The other end of the wicket was a peculiar mixture of sticks, cans and bottles.

The boundary to the left was the pub wall and the rule was if you hit the ball against the wall and someone caught the rebound with one hand, then you were out. To the right lay a less complicated and open landscape and four runs were four runs when the ball was hit beyond a patch of rose bay willow herb. Should someone slog the ball over the bowler's arm, we all prayed it would miss Mrs Scanlon's windows. Mrs Scanlon was a lady you should never upset. She was, indeed, a ferocious woman whose face looked as though someone had been cutting chips on it. She gave Frankie a real leathering last year when he incorrectly replayed a Denis Violet shot and accidentally increased the ventilation of her front parlour.

They appeared from nowhere. A ragged and unkempt posse, looking as though they would all benefit from a good scrub. They couldn't keep their hands off things, fiddling with Herbie's bike and swinging around Charlie's shiny new bat. Irene snatched the bike back from one of them, a lad named Eugene 'The Octopus' Mulcahy (for he had hands everywhere), and pushed it home. Eugene spoke in rapid, unintelligible sentences. His harsh Belfast accent would tear through your eardrums. He courted a devious reputation and made even his mother agree, he was someone who could crawl between your wall and its wallpaper and you wouldn't see it move.

The intimidation stopped when Lezzo called them to order. Preliminary negotiations between Frankie and Lezzo ended in them having first innings and Lezzo himself to open the batting.

'Who's opening yer bowlin'?' demanded Wally Duckworth, a freckled- faced youth, skilled at concluding his sentences with a strange nasal snort like an adenoidal pig.

'Our Ged!' I shouted back, though where my surprising courage came from I will never know.

'Your Ged?' blasted Lezzo. 'He's a cripple, in't he? A spaz! You lot have no chance if that's the best you can do.'

After his unconventional diagnosis of my brother's medical condition, Lezzo rejoined his army of urchins to broadcast the information. When their riotous laughter and derisive taunts had subsided, Lezzo confidently strolled up to the wicket to take the first ball.

I must have pushed Ged some twenty yards before we turned and began our run towards the wicket. I was now holding on to the wheelchair handles and running as fast as I could. Ged's right arm was swinging like the sails of a windmill in a gale. Round and round went his arm, you could feel the draught, and upon reaching the bowler's crease he released the ball.

Lezzo never saw it. It shaved his off stump by millimetres. I had let go of our Ged's chariot of fire to allow him his next manoeuvre, which was to steer himself away from the wicket and arrest his speed. Ged was a supremely skilled operator of his machine and casually applied the brake on one side and came to rest by skidding sideways in front of the visiting team. They had never witnessed such a display before. Each one of the ragged band of recidivists stood with their mouths open and bodies peppered with cinders. It was a turn of which Peter Craven, the Belle Vue speedway ace, would have been proud. Their muffled swear words were just audible and there was now a palpable mood change, from scornful and contemptuous ridicule to a numbness and confusion.

Lezzo too appeared visibly shaken by the delivery and immediately shouted,

'Is tharra corky (leather cricket ball) you're using?'

'Yerr, it is,' replied an excited Irene who had managed to stop the ball using a pair of her dad's welding gloves. 'Gorra problem?' she continued. Lezzo did not reply but nervously prodded the wicket with his bat. He'd obviously seen the professionals do it on the display television set in Jacobs Electrical Goods shop window. None of us had tellies, especially the Hanky Park clan.

I collected Ged and, on our journey back to the start point of his run-up, I said to him, 'Try dropping one short this time, Ged, give him a bouncer.' Ged chuckled with optimism and following that last delivery he was growing in confidence. We repeated the therapy, this time Ged's right arm was gyrating with a greater potency. We approached the crease at supersonic speed and Ged somehow raised himself out of his seat to gain height just before discharging the ball. You could hear the missile spin through the air. It did drop short of a length alright and bounced up to strike a rather surprised and unprepared Lezzo on the forehead. Everyone heard the crack of leather against bone.

There was a momentary stunned silence, followed by a session of protestation from our opponents, the worst of all being from Lezzo himself.

'Do one of them again and I'll kill ya!' he yelled, waving his bat like a deranged Tudor executioner.

Ged had completed his bowling routine with the customary skid in front of the visitors' pavilion. By this I refer to the railway wall on which they were lounging. Once more the sooty cinder barrage they received left them facially resembling Al Jolson.

However, for me it was Lezzo who appeared the most comical. By now he had a lump the size of a gobstopper on the front of his cranium, covered with a huge black smudge mark from the dusty ball. He reminded me of some anointed Catholic youth returning home from mass on Ash Wednesday.

It was all over for Lezzo on the next ball. He was clearly shaken by the recent attack on his visage and, in a desperate attempt to get out of the way but simultaneously trying to look cool, he slashed at the ball only to be 'yorked' (where the ball passes under the bat to hit the wicket) by our Ged.

The wickets rapidly started to fall. After as little as half an hour Lezzo's squad were all out for twenty-two runs, and eight of those were byes when Irene had to temporarily part company with us and collect her mum's divvy from the Co-op. Again, matriarchal power reigned supreme. You didn't argue with Irene and Alec's mum, if she said it was Wednesday on a Friday, then it WAS Wednesday.

Our response to their efforts was rather predictable. Frankie held on, scoring a few runs, most of them with thick edges. Herbie was quickly dismissed when he cowered and turned his back on one of Lezzo's violent deliveries. Alec tried a masterful forward defensive stroke, only to be beaten by his own anatomy as the ball went between his curved hind limbs, knocking down the beer crate.

Things started to improve when in at number five came our Ged. He could hold the bat in his right hand and slog a ball for miles. He was the doyen of wheelchair manoeuvrability, and jerky movements of his torso allowed him to shift the contraption in any direction. If he found a ball difficult to play, he would swing his chair across and block the ball with the spokes of his wheel. Complaints and remonstrations poured from the pugnacious Rossall Street bunch.

Cries of 'LBW!!' were instantly answered and defeated by our reply, 'Get lost! It didn't touch his leg!'

It gave me tremendous pleasure that the winning run should be scored by our Ged. He caught the ball right in the middle of the bat from a Rossall Street inswinger and it ricocheted off the pub wall and trickled down the ginnel. Ged dropped the bat and swiftly pushed his chair along the wicket to arrive at the opposite stumps and was greeted with the sound of rapturous applause and adulation.

Lezzo, now facially resembling a unicorn, responded to such a humiliating defeat by diving in amongst his fielders and belting some of them with the cricket bat, whilst simultaneously blurting abuse and profanities. Such bitter admonishment caused his troops to scatter in all directions. His lonely and demoralized figure turned to our Ged.

'Just you wait. There'll be a next time and I'll get ya good and proper,' he shouted, waving his fist. A humiliated figure then left the cinder croft stadium and moved back towards Hanky Park.

The following twenty minutes or so involved Frankie's match analysis, often reliving some of the more memorable moments. It was a great day and a spectacular triumph for our Ged and the Strawberry Road crew.

Our joy and merriment, however, was suddenly arrested when a concerned Charlie Sago inquired,

'Err............ Excuse me............ Has anyone seen my bat?'

Running Out of Steam

They were there every weekend in term time and practically every day during the school holidays. Boys wearing navy blue or grey gaberdine raincoats with a matching belt, stood huddled together. Each would sport a hand-knitted scarf, fashioned by a well-meaning female family member, and school caps would complete their cloned image. There were sometimes older youths whose seniority was reflected in a different dress code. They wore duffle coats and their hairstyles were less pudding basin or short back and sides. The quiff, cemented in place by dabs of Brylcreem, was true testimony of their maturity. Aged nine or nineteen was immaterial. These youngsters shared a common, committed and passionate pursuit.

Manchester Exchange station had a long through platform, so extensive indeed that the station embraced another, Manchester Victoria. Families taking their summer holidays to Morecambe would depart from here and, after five minutes into the journey, their kids would typically enquire,

'Are we there yet, Mam?'

'Are we there? Train's not reached th' end of t' platform yet. Now shut it!' came the flustered reply.

Its two thousand foot long stage, with room it seemed for the whole of the city population, saw this dedicated band of enthusiasts strategically positioned at the apex of this spur.

Some members of this cluster were armed with Brownie box cameras, some with binoculars, but all possessed a pencil and notepad. Elsewhere on their person, sometimes in the duffle bag carrying their fish paste sandwiches, or pushed into a coat pocket, was the passport that signified a true allegiance to the nowadays much maligned eccentricity of train spotting. The record manual championed by members of this fraternity was the Ian Allan Loco Spotter's Book. If your parents had a few bob then you would boast the hardback of this text, and this was a combined volume embracing all four regions of British Railways. Those of us with a less fortunate pedigree would have to make do with just the paperback edition of the LMS, which was less durable, and, after a year's frequent use, its worn pages resembled an exploded box of Izal toilet paper.

Train spotting was a magical pursuit for boys living in the age of steam railways. Each engine carried a visible number, and, if you were fortunate, a name. Engines were divided into classes and if you spotted one with a special modification, it undoubtedly improved your cachet with fellow enthusiasts. Hence, engine number 44766, a Stanier Class '5' 4-6-0 with a double chimney and Timken roller bearings, spotted at Longsight sheds, was worthy of tremendous praise. Catching sight of a Britannia Class 4-6-2, number 70001, and with its name – Lord Hurcomb, emblazoned on its windshields, made the group urge you to stand for Prime Minister.

Some of the younger and less seasoned spotters would often seek recognition and respect from the rest of the bunch. Seeing a 'Jinty' shunting coal at Eccles Junction, however, received little response from the bigger boys. Jinties were all too pedestrian in the North West. This quest for a sense of belonging to the group often forced these ten-year-olds to lie about sightings. Outrageous claims of witnessing a pair of 'Royal Scots' on the Manchester Ship Canal sidings were treated with contempt and ridicule. Didn't every train spotter know that 'Royal Scots' would never be found on that line? Scotties regularly serviced London, Crewe, Carlisle and Glasgow. The inhospitable Chat Moss was also the place to see them, as they pulled an army of coaches at hair-raising speeds to Holyhead or Llandudno.

So, when you were skilled in engine speak and could hold your own talking about Jubs, Black 5s, Super Ds, Crabs and Pacifics, as well as knowing train routes and timetables, you became a respected member of the loco-spotting fraternity.

In Eccles and Salford, you were never far from a railway line. The posse of train spotters to which I belonged would congregate at places such as Stott Lane, Cock Robin Bridge, Strawberry Road and the Four Bridges, Patricroft. These sites gave you a clear but somewhat distant view of the engines. Bridge positions were thoroughly enjoyable, because not only could you spot the train number on the smokebox plate as it hurtled towards you, but with a rapid run across the bridge and back again to achieve a side view, you could see if it was a 'namer'.

The next bridge experience was as 'hands on' as you could get. As the engine rattled its way under the bridge, you would be enveloped in a fog of smoke and steam. It was an intoxicating and addictive miasma for young boys despite its contents being carbon particles, oxides of sulphur and nitrogen, dioxins and vaporized oil. On a good day of spotting at the Four Bridges, you would return home grey from head to foot, looking as though you were destined for a chronic heart ward at the nearest hospital.

For many train spotters, viewing engines at a distance would be enough to satisfy their dependency. However, this landscape and remote experience proved inadequate and unsatisfactory for many intrepid loco zealots. Being able to touch a bogie wheel, stand on the footplate, closely scrutinize a tapered boiler, massage the grease on a set of bearings, or get oily hands from fondling a connecting rod, would go some way to medicate their loco fever. Therapy of this kind was only available in loco sheds.

Crewe and Longsight sheds involved a rail journey and, because we had little money, access to these destinations was only made available by the humble platform ticket. Catch the bus to Manchester Piccadilly station, buy a one penny platform ticket, and all pile on the next train. The knack was to avoid any guard or ticket inspector. Once at the other end of the journey, you would simply hop off the train, go to the end of the platform and nonchalantly stand on this spot as though you had been there all morning. It usually worked, although I do remember Morris Barlow feigning an attack of epilepsy whilst being interrogated by the station master. We'd pre-planned this response and Morris was a true thespian. His seizure was incredibly realistic thanks to baking powder he'd quickly placed under his tongue.

'Phone for an ambulance immediately!' cried Tommy Knox, 'He's dying!'

The alarmed superintendent panicked and ran along the platform to his office whilst we jumped on the 2.15pm to Marple. The orally-foaming Morris, of course, had no difficulty in getting a seat.

If you weren't rumbled by the platform staff, it was then time to dice with death. The engine sheds were usually a considerable distance from the station platforms and to reach these citadels of steam meant running across a sea of railway lines, some of it parallel fast track so that engines could pass stations in both directions at speed. Other lines curved, accessing the sheds or engineer's sidings. Looking across to the sheds from the platform, therefore, was a spaghetti-like landscape of track for you to negotiate.

We did it once at Crewe, but never again. The call to go was given us by Morris, the oldest boy in our troupe. Making certain all the signals were down, he waved his arm like Geronimo commanding his braves at The Little Big Horn. His braves were armed with pencils and notepad and all wore short trousers held up by a snake belt. Then we were off like a small army of rats scurrying across the rails and jumping over points. We were about halfway when we heard a metallic squeak as a signal to our right was quickly raised. Some track a few yards ahead of us suddenly shifted as a series of points switched, signifying an impending train. We all simultaneously froze and looked to our left. Coming straight at us was an express from Preston to Birmingham, New Street. It displayed an unyielding momentum as it hurtled along, leaving an almost horizontal plume of smoke in its wake. We all sensed its power as a compressed column of air crashed across our faces as the engine accelerated towards us. Four sharp shrills from the locomotive's steam whistle cut through the air, meaning we'd been spotted by the driver of this iron horse.

We returned to the platform with even greater speed than when we'd left it a couple of minutes before.

'Blinkin' heck, Morris, you nearly got us all killed!' shouted a visibly shaken Lenny Beswick.

'How was I to know that thing was gonna come round t' corner, Lenny. Anyroad, we're all ok, aren't we?' replied Morris, attempting to defend his captaincy.

'I've done it in me pants, Morris!' whispered the youngest member of our squad. It was eight-year-old, little Barry Mason. There was nothing of him at the best of times and now he was several ounces lighter.

The alarm raised by the crew on the engine's footplate sent a porter and the station master heading in our direction. Once more, it was time for Morris to give his audience yet another RADA performance, and so out came the baking powder to secure our liberty.

Following the Crewe sheds' debacle and the near extermination of the band of Salfordian trainspotters, the group unanimously agreed to practise its hobby closer to home. Morris suggested this course of action, yet his convincing declamation contained some curious and rather morbid logic. He argued that should any one of us be flattened by a passing train then it would be easier to notify their parents if we were closer to home. Morris always maintained a pragmatic perspective on life, or death, in this case.

Patricroft MPD (Motive Power Depot), a.k.a Patricroft sheds, was only a short walk from Eccles. Despite British Rail's efforts to keep uninvited citizens out of these steam engine houses, our disparate band of railway addicts found an easy access through an unlocked gate. We seemed immune to warning signs such as,

'UNAUTHORISED TRESPASSING IS HIGHLY DANGEROUS AND IS STRICTLY FORBIDDEN'

Sometimes before our assault on the sheds, we would sit on the wall and wave to the drivers, firemen and maintenance workers. More often than not they would return the gesture. They all seemed proud of their association with these agents of steam. We would often call out to them and ask what engines there were in the sheds. If they had time, they would call back the names and numbers of the locos. Little did they know that as soon as they disappeared we would be drawn inside this depot like flies to a sticky lolly.

The sheds offered repairs, cleaning and general maintenance. You would find all kinds of tradesmen there, such as blacksmiths, carters, loco cleaners and shunters. These enormous garages could house up to fifty engines. To the left of the new sheds was the magnificent seventy-foot long turntable, capable of waltzing huge tonnages of locomotives through one hundred and eighty degrees.

Dominating this engineering landscape was the coaling tower, an enormous vertical structure under which the tenders would sit and top up with coal. Its powerful winch was capable of drawing three hundred tons of coal up to its hopper. The tower stood six times as tall as an engine. Near the old sheds was the water tank and a chain would release much needed water life-blood into the engine tanks via a flexible leather pipe.

Standing on the wall opposite the sheds, or observing them from the iron bridge at the top of Nelson Street, you could witness many different forms of labour, all of which were accompanied by sounds of a shunting and coupling philharmonic orchestra:

Clunk, clank, clink, clunk........ clank... clank, clank, clunk, clink came the noises from the wagons' buffer plates in the shunting yards as they were herded and nudged into position by a 3F 'Jinty'. Such manoeuvres were achieved with the precision of a wily old sheepdog.

It was on one day of this typical railway industry that two of us penetrated the British Rail defences surrounding the sheds. We had heard that two engines, Assam and Oliver Cromwell, were undergoing a cleaning and servicing programme. News of this kind meant we had someone on the inside leaking such important secrets. Porky Percival, a rather chubby urchin who lived on Frobisher Street, had an 'uncle' who seemed to permanently reside with his mother. Uncle Bernie, as he was known to Porky, was a fireman who regularly worked on Britannia and Jubilee class engines, mainly on the Liverpool to Carlisle lines. Bernie would tell us stories of how he cooked eggs and bacon in the fire-box on a coal shovel as the engine thundered through the countryside. Older boys in the neighbourhood would jest that 'Uncle Bernie', as well as doing a high speed fry-up, was renowned for putting fire into many an old boiler, including Porky's mum.

It seemed too easy to slip into the sheds on that day. Not only this but as soon as we turned into the building we were faced with a magnificent shiny Class 5 engine and a namer too – 45156, the Ayrshire Yeomanry, standing in front of the Britannia we were really after, Oliver Cromwell. The feeling of being so close to these ambassadors of steam was all too much for my friend David. He broke sweat as he climbed onto this engine using the connecting rod and wheel as rungs of a ladder. He was all over the locomotive, running his hands over columns of rivets like a blind man reading Braille.

Being able to caress its nameplate and then stand on its footplate was a sensation better than United beating City on derby day, or opening presents on Christmas morning.

From the top of the footplate we could see all around the inside of the sheds. Standing on its own, away from the pedestrian Staniers, was an engine which pubescent locospotters would have sold their granny to see up close. It was a red Coronation class, the Duchess of Hamilton, in pristine condition sparkling in the afternoon sun. This princess of mechanical engineering was a real stranger to these parts and spotting it here meant that we could doubly underline it in red and date it in our record book. The urge to clamber all over its surface made us instantly leap down from the Brit class footplate and land on the clinker between the track.

Two huge hands the size of tennis rackets grabbed both of our collars. We were lifted off the ground and turned to face a man we certainly did not wish to meet. Bill Quigley was a huge block of a man. He was shed foreman and had a no-nonsense reputation for dealing with young trainspotters, who were the bane of his life. Rumour was that if you were caught by Quiggie, you faced torture and deportation. He purportedly despised kids more than WC Fields and his soubriquet amongst the rail workers at the depot was 'The King Herod of Patricroft.'

We were, of course, only nine years old and, in view of his demonic reputation, we were resigned to facing the possibility of the death penalty or maybe something even worse.

He carried us across the myriad of track like a gamekeeper swinging a brace of rabbits and finally dumped us rather unceremoniously on the floorboards in the corner of his office.

'Narthen, sit there, ya little buggers, while I phone for t' railway police and I'll ruddy well make sure ya both go ta prison,' he shouted.

'Ya could both have got thee sen' killed in them sheds, crushed to death or an arm ripped off, ya naughty little buggers! How old are thee?' he bawled. Neither of us could speak, our continuous sobbing muted any possibility of a reply.

He sat back in his chair and took out a penknife from his jacket pocket. His broad, stubby fingers then eased out its blade. We thought he was going to kill us there and then but instead, from his waistcoat he produced a stick of 'Twist' pipe tobacco, cutting it into small pieces before rolling them in his hands. Those same grubby digits packed his pipe with the resinous mass and then struck a match igniting the 'baccy' inside.

After what seemed a year of internment, the railway policeman arrived.

'I caught these two little blighters in the sheds, Ronnie. They could 'ave got 'emselves splattered across the track, crushed by t' foundry's steam hammer!' Quigley raised his voice and reinforced his gloomy prophecies by pointing at us with his pipe.

'Take 'em home and let t'parents deal wi' 'em and I hope they knock 'em into next week!' were Quiggie's final words.

Our whining and blubbering continued, not daring to look at Quiggie or the policeman. I was conscious of the fact that we were both huddled in the corner, our faces awash with tears and humiliatingly seated in two puddles of our urine.

'Here, hold up. Aren't you George Summerville's lad from t' cake shop on Regent Street?' inquired the policeman.

'Why? Does ter know him, Ronnie?' asked Mr Quigley.

'Aye, I do. He was in our outfit in North Africa and Italy. Aye, we went through a lot together did me and George. Leave it wi' me, Bill.'

The arrival of a railway police van outside the Eccles bakery caused some immediate concern and consternation amongst the small group of customers inside the shop. The tall policeman ushered us both into the premises. By that time we had both stopped crying, only to recommence our weeping at the sight of David's dad. A brief explanation from Ronnie and David received the biggest 'good hiding' from his dad I'd ever witnessed. It took place in front of customers, the shop assistant, the policeman and even made the angel cakes wince.

'I'll let your mam sort you out, Brian!' he shouted and we were both sent upstairs to the flat above the shop. My mum did sort me out and my gran even gave me a couple of bonus whacks for good measure.

Over the next two weeks we both decided we hated trainspotting, our parents, Eccles and Salford, Quiggie and the police force. We even contemplated getting jobs as cabin boys on one of the Manchester Liners we'd often seen along the Manchester Ship Canal. Our parents would eventually be informed of our whereabouts via David's Dan Dare toy radio station. Reluctantly, the decision was made to remain on *terra firma*, only because its batteries were flat and neither of us had any pocket money.

A letter addressed to 'Master David Summerville' was delivered to the cake shop. It was an invitation from the shed foreman for David and friend to have a supervised tour of the Patricroft locomotive sheds and enjoy, if possible, a short ride on the footplate of an engine within the confines of the shed. What a fabulous day! That infamous curmudgeon and child-hater, Quiggie, had arranged it all. God bless him.

That privileged friend was me.

The Sat'day Flicks

We always looked forward to Saturdays. Saturday morning would involve the weekly pilgrimage to the Essoldo cinema for what we called, 'The Thre'p'nny Crush'. A euphemistic alternative for such a gruesome term, however, was the Saturday morning children's pictures or 'the flicks'. The Essoldo was a cut above another cinema close to where we lived. The King's Picture House, situated two streets away, was affectionately known to locals as 'The Ranch' because it always showed cowboy films. It had dreadful wooden seats guaranteed to give you both bed sores and splinters. There was also a permanent aroma of urine throughout the premises.

The hundred and fifty strong contingent of Salford youths would queue noisily outside the grand building in all weathers until ten o'clock. A man in an ill-fitting, pin-striped suit would then let us in. The said person, a Mr Lucas, acted as major-domo and was supposed to provide effective crowd control by preventing skirmishes and the common practice of 'pushing in'. On weekdays and Saturday evenings he would don a red and grey overcoat and sport a peaked cap of similar colours, topped with gold braid. Such garments were supposed to give him status and authority. One Saturday morning he decided to wear this grand attire, only to receive humiliating comments from the pubescent gang in his charge. Embarrassing chants of:

'Oy, Field Marshall! Ain't it time to go in yet?'
'Let us in. Lord Nelson! It's chuckin' it down.'
'Someone's chucked scrambled egg on yer cap, Mister!'

Ridicule of such magnitude forced Mr Lucas to change his apparel on a Saturday morning and stick with his standard issue demob suit.

Another duty was for him to make sure everyone paid. On a Saturday morning there were two ladies in the ticket kiosk, who would frequently be overwhelmed by the eager punters.

'One at a time! One at a time! I've only got one pair of hands,' was their cry for order.

There were several youths who today could have escaped from Guantanamo Bay. Their regular routine of slipping around the kiosk maul and then hiding in the boy's toilets until the lights went down, was masterful. They would then confidently walk past the usherette and say,

'You saw me ticket when I came in with that lot.'

It was easy if Mrs Walkden was there. You could tell her you were the King of Siam and she'd believe you.

Once inside, there was always a scramble for seats. On occasions the balcony was placed out of bounds because of the previous week's escapades. Someone lobbed an ice cream cornet at the screen from the mezzanine. We all roared with laughter as it slowly trickled down the face of Hollywood star, Tex Ritter. On another occasion during the predictable western film, a sachet of itching powder was sprinkled on an unsuspecting group of brothers sitting immediately below. Kids viewing the film from several rows behind thought these boys were getting out of their seats and copying the Red Indian war dance being portrayed on the screen, unaware they were currently scratching themselves stupid.

Balloons, part-full of water, would become water bombs and gave many a ten-year-old a hair wash as one crashed against the rear of his cranium. This projectile was just one example of a huge arsenal of assault weapons fired by teenage bombardiers of the Fitzwarren Street artillery, seated some ten rows back.

Before the lights were dimmed Uncle Stan, the cinema manager and the person in overall control, would suddenly appear on stage. Stan Buckley was not a person to cross. He was a giant of a man with an extremely loud voice. His Claude Rains moustache and his bald head curiously jerked back and forth when he spoke. Someone's dad said it was a nervous tick he'd acquired when his unit had been relentlessly shelled at Caen.

Stan would always deliver the customary outline of the morning's programme, coupled with the expected chain of threats and punishments concerning misbehaviour. When he left the podium, the lights would dim and the roars from the juvenile fraternity would begin.

Control of the proletariat was down to the usherettes. Their principal weapon was the torch and their job was to detect and hopefully subdue any unrest from the masses. They wore yellow, three-quarter length, thin nylon coats lashed together with a belt, and would try to confiscate potato guns, pea shooters and catapults. We were better armed than the Khmer Rouge.

Several kids would start smoking and pass their Park Drive cigarette along the row to be shared by their mates. Smoking was not a hanging offence in those days. Everyone seemed to smoke. Certainly on screen, the likes of Paul Muni and Bogey (Humphrey Bogart), seemed permanently shrouded in a mist of tobacco smoke. At Saturday morning flicks, youngsters taking huge lungs full of carbon monoxide, was seen as more of a fire risk than them gambling with their health.

The remedial repertoire of reprimands from the usherettes, or majorettes as my friend Herbie would call them, ranged from an anaemic: 'Shhhhhhhhhhush!' to 'Eh, you in the specs! Pack it in.'

They often had more full-bodied admonishments, such as,

'I'll not tell yer again. Yes, you with the balaclava! Do that again and yer out!'

Perhaps the ultimate sanction of doom was when one of them would go and summon Mr Buckley. He would arrive and immediately ask,

'Right, who was it?'

The usherette would point to the miscreant and Mr Buckley would wade along a row of knees to grab hold of the felon. The defendant's instant protestations would include such classics as,

'It weren't me, Mister. It were him!'

Or,

'She's always pickin' on me, that woman. It's cos she don't like me mam.'

The scoundrel would then be dispatched down the stairs, across the foyer and thrown rather unceremoniously out onto the street. Mr Buckley would then lock the front door, dust himself down and return to his office and continue his amorous exploits with Mrs Tyldesley, the kiosk lady.

Watching a film with your mates was a most enjoyable experience. It was certainly a hands-on adventure, and by that I don't mean being grabbed by Mr Buckley. When the cowboy posse would gallop to give chase to the Indians, then so would we. The clatter of size fours on the cinema floorboards caused an awful din. On many an energetic chase even the projector would vibrate and make the likes of Tom Mix look as though he was suffering a seizure.

Audience participation was *de rigueur*. Uproarious cheers would break out when the goodies were seen chasing the baddies. Infectious boos and jeers would spread through the transfixed masses like an audible Mexican wave as the villain of the piece seized a defenceless woman. Pantomime cries of,

'Look out, he's behind yer!' echoed through the auditorium as our entranced viewers attempted to save their hero.

One mishap guaranteed to cause trouble at t' mill was when the film in the projector snapped. Because of the lack of celluloid, the screen would instantly glow as bright as the sun, only to be followed by complete darkness as the projectionist turned off his offending machine. This would immediately precipitate stamping on the floor, big time. Such plantar indiscipline would be accompanied by boos, followed by simultaneous single claps.

'Why are we waiting? Why are we waiting? Oh, why are we waiting?' chanted the unruly patrons. The melody to which these enquiries were sung was the carol, 'Oh Come, All Ye Faithful.'

The masses were only placated when the frenzied repairs of the projectionist allowed transmission to be restored. Lengthy interruptions of the performance meant a re-emergence of Mr Buckley, whose attempts to remain calm yet authoritarian would fail. This resulted in him giving a performance in volume and rhetoric akin to Hitler at the Nuremberg Rally.

There would always be an intermission, when it was hoped the sales of ice cream tubs would bring in extra revenue. It also meant you could leave your seats and harry the usherettes, who now wore a halter which bore the weight of the tray of ice creams and lollies. Once more there was little crowd control and regular scrummages around these ladies would spawn theft, assault and bad language as the vending process continued.

I always thought ice cream tubs were a rather foolish item to sell at Saturday morning cinema. Admittedly, the ice cream tasted delicious, but you were left with the wooden spoon, the receptacle plus its lid. Spoons were then used in the second half as catapults, flicking all sorts of debris at nearby entranced viewers. The tubs and lids, having been licked dry of their contents by the malnourished army, were then thrown at someone or trodden into the floor for some hapless cleaner to collect as they prepared the auditorium for that night's show.

During winter months, when the audience had queued outside for long periods in the rain, the air inside the cinema was distinctly frowsty as the warm room allowed us to vaporize the rainwater on our clothing. This, mixed with stale sweat, greasy hair, halitosis and flatulence, produced a rancid yet unique atmosphere unknown to research chemists.

The plots of most of the films we watched were predictable. Nevertheless, we sat there transfixed as the baddy chased the goody and then vice versa. The tendency was to chop protracted films in half, just at the point when the action reached a crescendo. This would act as bait to entice the kids back the following week to see what happened. Logic of this nature regularly backfired, as the captivated viewers did not take well to the action stopping and being informed 'Continued Next Week'. Unrest from the natives manifested itself as cries of disappointment, whistles and banging of seats. It would usually upset the juvenile audience for the rest of the performance.

The whole experience would finish after a couple of hours. The lights would go up and then mass hysteria would prevail. Children would noisily scramble out of their seats, some leaving the way they had entered the building. The majority of urchins in the front and rear stalls would, however, push open the fire doors and burst out onto the side street and back alley. The premises were completely vacated within a couple of minutes. Usherettes had unsuccessfully prevented escape from this prohibited exit, but seemed relieved that it was all over for another week. Mrs. Tyldesley was frequently seen readjusting her dress following Mr Buckley's physiotherapy session.

I once hung back with my friend Herbie to note down the times of the main feature film that evening and I overheard Mr Buckley say to his red-faced concubine:

'You know, Vera, I often pray for The Pied Piper of Hamelin to visit Salford ...... I hate kids.'

The Tripe Cart

My school cap had some use, I suppose. If I tilted my head forward, the rain would smash against it rather than pepper my face and make it sore. The journey from the top of our street to the shop took a couple of minutes. My mum was already there, six o'clock, as regular as a prune-eating vegan.

'Now, don't forget Brian, don't let him diddle you out of trotters like he did yesterday. We were one short. Count the boxes, there should be three,' she advised.

'You have to watch him, he's a crafty one is that Harry Modley. I don't want Mrs.Whitehead thinking I'm on the rob when it's that thievin' devil. Anything I can't account for comes out of my wages and I don't intend lining his pockets either. So think on, love.'

This barrage of advice and frustration was administered as my mother commenced dressing the shop window. The UCP tripe shop was an essential inclusion for any town in the North West. The acronym was for United Cattle Products and each emporium sold a comprehensive range of bovine and porcine viscera. Tripe would lie next to haslet, cowheel adjacent to elder. Savoury ducks - a form of faggot (which neither resembled nor tasted like ducks) - nestled close to black pudding and pigs' trotters.

The marble display counter would then be fine tuned with packs of white dripping - a cardiologist's nightmare - separated by tufts of plastic parsley. My mother's efforts at shop window display of this varied selection of offal was a credit to her creative skills. The results were matched only by the likes of Kendal Milne in terms of presentation, appeal and magnetism. Kendal's was Manchester's quality department store, selling clothes, homeware and furniture. You only visited Kendal's if you had a few bob. Consequently, most people from Pendleton did not have these premises on their calling cards; the wares of a UCP tripe shop were, however, certainly within their budget.

Tripe is a cow's stomach and can manifest itself in many forms. The best cut in my mind was seamless or blanket tripe. It was lovely to eat raw and there was no finer summertime meal than tripe and chips, the tripe being seasoned with salt and vinegar. A dash of pepper and a couple of tomatoes gave it that extra piquancy. We lived on tripe scraps – perks of the job. Honeycomb and thick seam were different parts of the stomach and not for the faint-hearted. A chunk of thick seam made your jaws ache. My mate Herbie was given a portion by my mum and he said he was still chewing it after two weeks. Many people boiled it with milk and onions, but that was for wimps. Raw was best.

Black tripe was a delicacy. It was a sheep's stomach and, as the name suggested, was a dark grey colour. It was easy to chew and had a unique flavour. We had that once a fortnight. For me it was just as much *haute cuisine* as is *cassoulet* to a French peasant farmer.

My only complaint about tripe is that it always came from the factory in heavy wooden boxes. These were extremely weighty when full of tripe or cowheel, and it was my job to collect them with a tripe cart from the delivery wagon at Salford market. The tripe was also soaked in a generous suspension of starch that would leak from the boxes and stain everything white that it touched. This included my trousers and shoes. After the long haul from the market back to the shop, my shoes were as white as a pair of cricket boots and I was now wearing polka dot trousers. Such sartorial accessories meant I always received a huge dose of sarcastic and hurtful comments from fellow pupils at my school.

'Hey up, the snowman cometh!' shouted Philip Baxter.

'Are you opening t' bowling, Bri? But it's not t' cricket season?' mocked Dave Morgan.

The white stains on my trousers also precipitated embarrassing jibes about indulging in too much self-pleasure. All in all, a humiliating start to any school day.

'It's a rotten morning, put that shop coat on and mind what I've told you about checking the delivery,' she repeated.

I hated this part of the day. It wasn't too bad in the summer, but this time of the year was certainly no pleasure. I donned the coat, pulled the peak of my cap down and opened the back door of the shop into the yard. There, waiting for me, was my offal conveyance catalyst, the tripe cart. It was a broad contraption and three-quarters my size. Two large wooden wheels, two long metal handles and the timber carrying frame completed its structure. It was hardly a vehicle from which you would gain any cachet as you trundled along Broad Street in the direction of Salford market.

Pushing the cart was hard enough work when it was empty. I could get it through the back gate unless it was windy. On those occasions it would blow back on me and slam shut. Sometimes it took as many as four attempts to beat the door and complete this frustrating manoeuvre.

Croft Street was cobbled and required plenty of push to get the cart up the slope to the road. I'd charge at the incline and hope to gain enough momentum to reach the top. The wooden cartwheels rattled as they struck the cobbles and then waved from side to side. This lack of streamlining forced the cart to lose energy as I made a determined assault onto the top of the street. My body would shudder and share a synchronized resonance with the cart, my lower jaw jumping around and my arms trembling against the metal handles. Passers-by must have assumed I was a sickly boy prone to seizures.

There was always little traffic around at that time in the morning and I could take advantage of the smooth tarmac along Broad Street. A five-minute push would see me arrive at Cross Lane. This thoroughfare was the main artery linking Pendleton to Salford Docks. Manchester was now a port and these docks marked the termination of that amazing piece of civil engineering, the Manchester Ship Canal.

There was an unwritten law about the pubs along Cross Lane. The closer they were to Broad Street, the less likely you were to get your throat cut on a Saturday night. Putting it another way, should you decide on a few pints in a pub closer to the docks, then you must have a record of the blood group to which you belong somewhere on your person.

Pub singers, such as 'The Gorgeous Lita Delroy', a.k.a Elsie Perkins, would perform no further down Cross Lane than The Cattle Market Public House.

'I want wages for me singin', not hospitalization,' was Lita's rationale.

It was on Cross Lane, about a year before, that I saw the first black Salford resident. Cess, everyone called him. Apparently Cess was a merchant seaman who had jumped ship at Pormona Docks some years before. Despite visiting Samoa, The Seychelles and many other enchanting places around the world, Cess had come to the decision that a mid-terrace on Ladysmith Street, Ordsall, was to be his Shangri- La. There he was happily cohabiting with Doreen Broadbent, a former 'lady of the evening' with whom he had spent many an enjoyable hour.

Never having seen a black person before, kids visiting the area for the first time would rudely stare at him. Cess didn't seem to care.

Just before you reached the market was The Salford Hippodrome. I was fascinated reading the names of 'artistes' on the billboards. Vaudeville took some time to die in the North West, before the cinema and then television became the principal forms of entertainment. Acts such as,

'Zelda — The world's only female topless ventriloquist', was, I heard, extremely popular. The blokes in the audience would say they never saw her lips move.

'Richie Lofthouse — The Ancoats' Matt Monro'.

'The Brothers Zagreb, Acrobats Extraordinaire' — Watch Them Build the Human Pyramid'. A rather bizarre accomplishment, I thought, since there were only two of them.

And

'The Great Marvo, The Memory Man'.

These were but a few of the big names currently playing 'The Salford Hipp'. It seemed ironic that Marvo failed to arrive at the venue one evening, claiming he'd completely forgotten about the booking.

I was relieved that my journey to the market was early in the morning and most of my mates weren't awake.

Dougie Douglas was though. He had a paper round.

'Dosser!' he would shout as he ran past me. He used this endearment every day. He was hardly a prince of verbiage. No wonder he didn't pass the eleven plus.

I dreaded the thought of bumping into Ernie Melia. Ernie was a most unsavoury youth, who worked for his dad on the market. He rarely attended secondary school and had more days sick than Andy Capp. My gran referred to him as 'a nasty piece of work' and always said that she wouldn't trust him as far as she could throw him. I thought this a rather obvious statement for he weighed eighteen stones and she only eight. This morning, though, he got me.

'Eh! Eh! Rag bone! Rag and bone kid! Oy, don't try 'n' run off, I've seen yo!'

Ernie spoke with a broad Salford patois. He continued,

'Yer, gerrof, kid cos I'll chuck a dirty big ducker at yo!'

For the uninitiated and those unfamiliar with Salford-speak, he implied he was going to hurl a large stone in my direction.

I didn't say anything. I knew what he could do. Just keep your head down and keep pushing the cart. Today, in these early hours, and to my good fortune, Ernie had bigger fish to fry.

At the entrance to Salford market there was a large open area where the market traders would park their wagons. It was part of the former cattle market. At 6.30 am the tripe cart boys would assemble to take their early deliveries from Harry Modley. There were usually five of us, though two were hardly boys. Eddie Gleason and Mr Patterson were ancient and in their forties, doing the job for extra beer money. One lad who pushed the Irlams o' th' Height cart, had furthest to go. He was a muscular sixteen-year-old and could run like a gazelle. He would take no lip from Harry and, as soon as he'd loaded up, he was off with such a speed it was as though he was suffering from an overdose of 'opening medicine' (a trusted laxative, guaranteed by pharmacists to 'put a road through you').

I used to talk to one of 'the boys', Raymond Eckersley. He ran the Regent Road cart. Raymond was a pleasant yet nervy lad, about my age and, like me, his mother ran a similar shop off the bottom of Cross Lane. He had a stammer but would bravely attempt long sentences. We would both discuss how we hated the job and that we shared a mutual dislike of Harry Modley. Once, he retaliated at one of Harry's caustic comments about Ray's colourful balaclava his mum had knitted with left-over bits of wool.

'Ya look a reet nancy boy in that, Ray! Like one o' them homos!' Harry cruelly jibed.

'B..b..b..b..b,' stammered Ray. But, before he could finish his words, Harry was in the driver's cab and away.

The final cathartic return of 'B..b..b..b..b..bugger, b-bugger off, Harry!' was finally delivered as the wagon shot off in the direction of Manchester, and Harry was none the wiser.

Ray would stand with his hands in his pockets and nervously fiddle with his privates as we waited for the wagon to arrive. When it finally did chug around the corner, belching diesel everywhere, both the intensity and frequency of his anxious fiddles increased.

The two old men were always served first. Harry was as nice as pie with these two. Nothing was too much trouble. Then the gazelle stepped in for his order and soon disappeared in a vapour trail towards Pendleton Church.

'What's your order, Ray? Oh for God's sake, don't try and tell me it, lad, we'll be 'ere all t' ruddy day. Just give us t' docket. I've got to be in Bury by half seven.' Harry was a real charmer.

Ray's self-prescribed genital comfort, designed to help him cope with his unease and insecurity, quickly terminated when Harry reminded him,

'Reet lad, that's you done — and ruddy well leave yerself alone. Yer'll rub it off!'

It was my turn next. I passed him the ticket and watched him move the boxes of tripe.

'That's one o' honeycomb, one o' thick seam, two o' blanket and one o' black,' shouted Harry as he tossed them onto the cart. Occasionally, some of the tripe would slip out of the box and slide across the back of the wagon. Any loose pieces would be stabbed rather unceremoniously with a pitch-fork and dropped back into the container.

'I want me box of cowheel and four o'trotters too, Harry, ya know?' I bravely called.

'Alright, I've only got one pair of hands, lad!' retorted a flustered Harry. I made sure the boxes were full and on board.

'What yer rummagin' at?' he growled.

'Me mum says I've got to check it's all there. You dropped us short last time.'

'Short? Short? I never did, ya cheeky bugger. It's her who can't add up. Anyway, for sayin' that, tell her I won't give her that big kiss next time I see 'er.'

God! The thought of him kissing my mum?

Harry was, indeed, in a rush this morning. He pushed the order into his top pocket without scrutinizing the last part of the invoice.

'Reet, I'm runnin' a bit late. Bury, here I come!' and with that he started the engine, showering the contents of my cart with a carbon mist.

Yes, I'd done it. I'd got that box of trotters back. My mum would be ecstatic. I pushed that cart as hard as I could back to the shop, occasionally looking over my shoulder in case Harry had realized his error and was coming back to reclaim the extra box of offal.

Dropping down into Croft Street at speed was a life-threatening manoeuvre and I narrowly avoided flattening Mrs Crossley as she went off to work.

'Hell fire! Ya could 'a' killed me. Yer great lummock!' I heard her shout as I crashed through the open back gate with so much momentum I nearly finished up in the back of the shop.

'Steady on, our Brian! Who's chasing you?'

I couldn't have told her even if there was. It took me ages to catch my breath.

'I've got yer box of trotters, mum, that Harry short-changed you on yesterday,' I gasped and waited for praise and adulation.

'You what, love?' she enquired. 'Harry's just dropped one off at the shop on his way to Bury. He said he was sorry and it must have been a mistake.'

Oh, bloomin' heck. What have I done?

'Did he give you a kiss, mum?' I enquired with deep concern.

'Who? Harry? Goodness me, chuck, I'd rather have all me teeth pulled out than let him kiss me,' she joked as she ruffled my hair. 'Come on and have your breakfast.'

'It's not tripe again is it, mum?' I enquired.

'No, it's your favourite. Black puddings and mustard. That'll warm you up,' she said as she opened the oven door.

I consumed the congealed pig's blood morsels with the appetite of a deranged vampire and, after licking the final traces of mustard off the plate, I remembered I faced two problems.

How did I get the extra box of trotters back? But, perhaps more important than that, how was I going to live down going to school wearing freshly chequered black and white trousers and those white shoes again?

Pengy Baths

I recall a fellow pupil once clearing a school chemistry laboratory by over-producing chlorine gas. His intended test-tube volume of the stuff continued to pour out of the apparatus, and a poisonous green haze soon gripped each part of the room whilst simultaneously seizing the throats of his fellow aspiring chemists. We subsequently found ourselves desperately fighting for the doors and windows to avoid being certified dead by misadventure. The school caretaker, Mr Flynn — already an asthmatic — nearly went to the great broom cupboard in the sky as he attempted to switch on a decrepit fume cupboard that demonstrated all the suction of a blocked toilet.

Chlorinated lime, when added to water, undergoes a gradual chemical change and evolves litres of this toxic gas. The store-room of Pendleton (Pengy) Baths contained sacks of this powder, stacked on pallets. The water in the pool was often so green with chlorine it looked as though you were swimming in a sea of pea soup. Emerging from this water you would dry yourself, get dressed and return home smelling strongly of bleach for up to a fortnight.

Chlorine is a powerful agent, capable of killing most things from bacteria to school caretakers. The practice was to saturate the water in the swimming pool with chlorine early in the day, before the proletariat were allowed in. There was a noticeable lack of quantitative control for measuring the amount of chlorinated lime added. Pool attendants would toss hundredweight sacks of this powder into the water until it looked, quote: 'green enough'. This emerald hue was the Health and Safety benchmark for the pool supervisors of Pengy Public Baths in the 1950s. Chlorine gas would also be produced more rapidly if the water was acidified. This acidification process was easily achieved thanks to youthful bathers urinating undetected into the pool water. After a morning's immersion in this chemical cocktail, invigorated swimmers would leave these premises with iridescent bloodshot eyes and a general air of being the most aseptic object on the planet.

The building typified Victorian architecture and its red brick façade clearly distinguished it from the adjacent warehouses. The rouge of the brickwork was subdued by years of exposure to a sooty, damp atmosphere that clung to its surface. The address of the establishment was etched into the grey limestone pediment over the entrance. It read:

'Pendleton Public Baths'

Indeed, one important function of this Salfordian property was to provide a place where members of the community could come along for a bath. Few houses in Hanky Park had a bathroom and any major body lavage took place in galvanized bathtubs in front of the fire. For the sum of sixpence at Pendleton Baths, you were given a towel and a bar of carbolic soap and directed to a room containing a row of tiled baths serviced by chrome-plated bath taps. There you could rid yourself of the layers of grime that had accumulated on your skin and hair over the last couple of weeks (or months, depending on how hard up you were).

Particularly on winter days, Pengy Baths was the place to go. It offered warmth, recreation and exercise for the children of the locality. Entrance to the building was by a series of steps and on the left was a kiosk where you paid your sixpence. A noisy turnstile separated you from the door leading to the pool area. It was threepence more if you wanted to hire a towel. This optional extra was white with 'Property of Salford City Council' emblazoned in red letters on its surface. There was a design fault with these sundries, in that they seemed to repel water and have zero absorbency. Their squeegee-like property simply moved water droplets from one part of your body to another.

There was always a feeling of anticipation and adventure about going swimming. You became aware of a distant babble of excitement and hysteria coming from behind the broad wooden doors leading to the pool. This hubbub changed to a deafening tumult as these doors were opened and you witnessed hundreds of youngsters enjoying their immersion in the green water. The splashing noises made by hundreds of eager children thrashing around, was equivalent to that of standing by the Victoria Falls.

Frequently the pool was so congested with bodies that there was standing room only. Such space limitation forced you to either jump up and down or simply stand there and splash yourself with water. On these occasions swimming was impossible, except at the deep end. However, this area was principally colonized by older boys and was off limits to water babies. Doing the breaststroke across a width of the pool in this territory was a dangerous practice, since you were in mortal danger of being crushed by an irresponsible simpleton who had suddenly decided to leap from the high diving board. Indeed, this structure seemed to attract the psychopaths and deranged members of the community.

On either side of the pool were the changing cubicles. The regulation was boys on the left and girls on the right. Your modesty was protected by a sheet of tarpaulin, tied at the top with canvass strips. Once you untied these tapes, the waterproof cover would roll down and members of the public were then free to get changed hidden from bathers. It always seemed to be when you had just removed your underpants, and your genitalia and bottom were exposed, that some cretin would run along the side of the pool pushing against each of the covers. Bathers would then get an eyeful of your nether parts and, on particularly cold days, your microscopic willy would provide humiliating ammunition for the girls when you eventually climbed into the water.

It was compulsory for bathers to visit the footbath before going into the main pool. The purpose of this medicated structure was to deal with the exudations from sweaty feet and to destroy fungi and other micro-organisms. The floor of this contraption always seemed covered in coarse black silt, fragments of toenails and plasters. Most people were of the opinion that you emerged from the footbath with more debris and pathogens than when you first stepped into the thing.

The chemistry of the main pool water was designed to deal with disease. There were kids whose bodies were daubed in gentian violet, a commonly used lotion designed to treat sores, fungal infections and lanced boils. Athlete's foot, ringworm and the dreaded verrucae were ailments you would frequently contract following an afternoon's visit to the baths. Indeed, it was a wonder plague and typhus weren't also on the menu. On occasions, your swim was interrupted by a passing buoyant turd colliding with your ear, its size being in proportion to its perpetrator. Petite stools were once the property of small children, whilst larger deposits emanated from teenage donors. Taking a mouthful of this suspension was not recommended and the presence of vomited peas and pieces of carrot in the water was further testimony to its disagreeability.

In the days before The Clean Air Act, sunlight seldom kissed the pavements of Salford streets. Consequently, the bodies jumping around in the pool were blanched and skinny. This lack of pigmentation was enough to give you snow blindness. Children, whose ribcages were as prominent as toast racks, merrily played with others whose skin bore after-effects of pimples, bed bugs and psoriasis.

There were few fat children although the ironically named twins, William and Elsie Large, both weighing in at fifteen stones, were frequent visitors to Pengy Baths. Their mother would explain their corpulence as glandular complications, though no mention was made of their predilection for bread and dripping and sugar butties. The Archimedes theory of water displacement was particularly relevant whenever the Large twins visited the premises. The pool was topped up with several litres following their departure.

Many of the bathers wore woollen swimming trunks or costumes. These characters were forever pulling them up as the garments absorbed water. When they emerged from a 'splash about' and stood shivering on the pool's edge, their trunks would sag around the crotch as gravity shifted the water downwards. Consequently it looked as though they were incontinent as the wool garment emptied its water content onto the floor. Diving in was also a problem for any Johnny Weissmuller wearing woollen trunks, since he would expect to part company with them as his body cut through the water.

Order within the confines of the swimming baths was the responsibility of the three pool attendants, each armed with a whistle. Poor behaviour was highlighted by a single blast from this instrument. Serious breaches of discipline were marked by several short blasts followed by a more protracted burst; the length of this final toot being proportional to the magnitude of the offence. Hence, when Stephen Modlinski would whack fellow swimmers with his prosthetic hand that he would frequently detach and use as a weapon, this merited two rapid sonic shafts. Stephen was an excellent swimmer who insisted on removing his prosthesis before tearing through the water. Sadly he was of no use whatsoever at school swimming galas, because his lack of symmetry meant he couldn't swim in a straight line.

Dive bombing from the top board also received a similar single whistle response. Fighting or attempting to drown someone would always qualify for the longer blasts, followed by expulsion from the premises.

Mrs Toomey, a dour lady with simian features, looked after female discipline whilst Nobby Clarke and 'Vinny' Armitage dealt with the boys. Nobby was a man in his sixties who waddled along the poolside. His strange gait, caused by an arthritic hip, was mimicked by many of the young pool patrons. They would walk in a line behind him, all swaying from side to side, and the troupe resembled a mother duck with her siblings.

'Vinny', whose real name was John, was in his thirties. His nickname 'Vinny' was given to him by his mates after he shot away most of his right ear on Sword Beach during the D Day landings. The firing chamber of his standard issue Lee Enfield rifle exploded as he attempted to finish off the inhabitants of a pillbox who then ran off, unable to believe their good fortune. The nickname 'Vinny' was, of course, taken from a similar aurally-challenged gentleman, Vincent Van Gogh.

The attendants wore white overalls and their feet were shod with clogs, ideal footwear for the wet terracotta tiles along the poolside. They had access to a long wooden pole, intended to drag out debris that would often block the grill on the floor of the deep end. Bits of perished goggles, hair, punctured water wings, a plimsoll, hair clips were common examples of such jetsam. The insoluble mass was cemented in place around this grid by all forms of detritus.

You were given a coloured rubber wrist-band when you paid your entrance fee. This colour-coded bracelet identified your recreational time allowance in the baths. To prevent pool congestion, the attendant – usually Wally Turner, for he had the loudest voice – blew his whistle and would then bellow:

'Right, yellow bands, everyone out!'

The majority of yellow banders would vacate the pool and make their way to the changing cubicles. Those recalcitrant members of the same colour, determined to gain some extra swimming time, would either remove their band and shove it inside their trunks or attempt to hide against the wall of the pool out of view. Wally was a seasoned campaigner and wise to most avoidance schemes. He also knew his clientele and the recidivists likely to try his patience. A quick blast with a powerful high-pressure hosepipe, as effective as a water canon, soon dislodged these stubborn souls.

I once attended the baths only to find it half- full of water, not bathers! I remember it did not seem to bother the swimmers much at all, though the sensation of jumping into the water at the deep end was rather like throwing yourself off the Hoover dam.

It was the noise of the kids in the pool that added to the excitement. Splashing, thrashing, slapping water produced a constant tinnitus and conversations between bathers were loud and brief.

'Go on! Dive bomb. I dare ya!'

'Chuck him in!'

'Pack it in or I'll kill ya!'

'Christ! Ya nearly drowned me!'

This high-pitched *lingua franca* cut through the damp air already saturated with the distinctive sounds of the bathing process.

Bringing along a snorkel to the pool illustrated two things about you, incredible naivety and a willingness to court drowning. The sight of a small plastic tube poking out of the water seemed to urge even the most timid of individuals to tamper with it. The action of placing your palm over its exposed lumen, momentarily asphyxiated the swimmer, usually causing a cessation of his motion through the water. The meddling perpetrator was then given a 'thick ear' by the drownee, as long as there was not a huge difference in their size. More sadistic and over-zealous attempts involved bashing the top of the device with a clenched fist. This aggressive interference usually ripped the rubber mouthpiece out from behind the swimmer's lips, along with a couple of teeth. As a by-product of this action, the distressed budding Jacques Cousteau inhaled a lungful of water and then had to be helped out of the pool by a friend.

Performing the breaststroke or crawl proved to be all too boring for a number of patrons. The element of 'dare' usually arose towards the end of a swimming session. The girls were worse than the boys at suggesting daring deeds. Simple tasks of seeing how long you could hold your breath under the water, or doing a handstand in the shallow end, were replaced by more heroic provocations. Somersaulting from the top diving board, or back flips after a chain of bounces from the springboard, gave way to acts of sheer lunacy. I recall one red-haired urchin climbing up into the public gallery and being goaded into action by a crowd of onlookers below. The madcap responded positively to taunts of:
    'Yeller belly! Yer a yeller belly mardarse! Jump! Jump!'

The pale youngster launched himself from the gallery like a puffin leaving a cliff face and landed with an almighty crash into the deep end. This intrepid, yet irresponsible act was unfortunately observed by not only the human components of the pool, but also by Nobby Clarke and the ape-like Mrs Toomey. I have never heard so much whistling from these two supervisors. Nobby did a high-speed waddle along the poolside, armed with a huge lance with a loop at its apex. In a no-messing manoeuvre, Nobby hoiked the nine-year-old out of the water, clouted him and sent him to get dressed, only to throw the lad out onto the street one minute later. We were aghast when the partially-clothed boy, who had only managed to put on his shorts and had only one arm in his shirt, was being swung through the air by Nobby. Mrs Toomey walked behind carrying the kid's shoes, pullover and socks. The waif landed ungraciously on the pavement, wearing about as much clothing as Sabu, the Elephant Boy.

A brief silence spread through the room, only to be broken when Nobby returned bellowing,

'Right, I don't care what ruddy colour band you have — I want every bugger out, now! Every bugger, out!'

He then proceeded to pace up and down the poolside like an expectant father, pushing semi-clad juveniles out of the building, including me.

I wouldn't have minded being punished like this under normal circumstances, but I had only just paid my sixpence to get in.

Father Brennan

A fierce and ruddy complexion made his face appear like the skin of a red Desiree potato. For years this rough and inflamed surface had been blasted by rain straight from the Atlantic. Its abrasive colour and varicose lines were intensified by his predilection for Bushmills. The shame of it, a Catholic priest drinking Protestant whiskey.

Father Brennan was a Kerry man whose first ministry took him away from his birthplace to Lettermullan, a wild and lonely outpost along the Connemara coast. Such a remote placement did nothing to work against his personal desire for a sense of detachment from his parishioners. Since his ordination, his long-standing ideology was to ensure his flock upheld their faith but to communicate with them only when it was absolutely necessary.

It was, indeed, a miracle when the shock of him being redeployed to St James' in Hanky Park, Salford, failed to secure a premature meeting with his celestial superintendent. The man of few words believed it a punishment from The Almighty for patronizing the Antrim distillery.

He joined the St James' team during my confirmation year. My gran was a staunch Catholic and insisted the correct thing for me was to follow the celebration of my First Holy Communion with a final commitment to the religion as a confirmed left-footer. At her insistence I was bought an ill-fitting suit from the catalogue, a new white shirt (that would also do for school), a hideous kipper tie and a pair of black shiny shoes with plastic soles. In full regalia, if someone had given me a violin case, I would have looked less out of place at the St Valentine's Day massacre than at a service inside Salford Cathedral.

Communicant youths were required to attend Confession. This was held on a Saturday afternoon, the aim being to confess and do penance for your sins. The slate now wiped clean meant you could receive Communion at mass next day. Everyone in the local community, even the adults, hoped Father Brennan would not be behind the grating taking Confession. The purging you received from him would keep you in the church at least half an hour. You instantly knew it was he by the curious aroma of Capstan Full Strength and sweaty feet slowly effusing through the trapped air inside the cubicle. Once seated in the confessional, there would be silence.

In an attempt to kick start dialogue, I would always say,

'Forgive me, Father, 'cos I have sinned.'

There was still nothing from the other side of the grille, just the sound of laboured breathing. This in itself would always unnerve me. The sensation was like waiting for a loud banger to go off on Bonfire Night. You just weren't too sure for how long the fuse would burn.

I would then continue,

'I have told lies, Father, and on occasions I have sworn, Father. Oh, and last week I didn't get the coal up from the cellar for me gran even though she asked me three times, Father.'

Then it came — three loud shafts of denunciation, some of it incomprehensible due to his sharp Kerry brogue. All I knew was I'd upset him and my immediate liberty would be curtailed repenting for my sins.

'Twenty Our Fathers, twenty Hail Marys and ten Glory Bes. Now, away you go and fear God's wrath!' he shouted.

Leaving the confessional was like walking into a dentist's waiting room. His assembled clients, seated in pews close to the consultation chamber, appeared terrified, and now even more alarmed by the verbal salvo I had just endured.

There would be some youngsters for whom this was all too much. They would return home laden with sin and add yet another venial transgression to their collection by informing their parents that Father Brennan had been ill that day.

Like many of us, I always decided not to tell him everything. He was not the kind of man to whom you could really offload. Terrible sins, such as playing with myself, were best unmentioned. I had witnessed his apoplexy when a naïve Gerard Wilson confessed he'd seen his Auntie Edna naked and had quite enjoyed the experience.

I always imagined my soul as a white fluffy cloud tainted with black spots. Each spot represented a sin and, following my stint inside the confessional, I would emerge with a soul as white as a cumulus on a summer's day, except for several engrained mortal sin blotches commemorating my frequent attempts at self-pleasure.

The trouble was trying not to perpetrate other sins between the time of leaving Confession and taking Communion the next day. Rita Unsworth always found it difficult to fulfil such dedication. Rita was a large-chested girl who lived opposite us. She would improve her financial position on the way home from church by generously offering the tumescent upper areas of her anatomy to a group of precocious urchins at the top of Jubilee Street. At 'one penny a feel', a homeward-bound purchase of a bottle of Dandelion and Burdock presented her with little fiscal challenge and gave change to boot.

Sunday mass was compulsory for all practising Catholics. Catholicism and commitment to the religion was serious business in those days. Father Brennan, as head honcho at St James', ran the parish on similar lines to Ho Chi Minh. He would dispatch his junior priests, Fathers Wood and Dougan, to relay his displeasure with families having a poor church attendance record. Their God-fearing response was to instantly improve weekly church visits and then lapse again a month or so later. I can only recall one occasion when the man himself made a house call. It was to the O'Rourke family in Lord Nelson Street. A small crowd gathered opposite the house as Father Brennan knocked on the door with all the determination of 'the club' man coming to collect an instalment. The meeting was quickly concluded, and his voice, which my mother said could cut through glass, was heard making Mrs O'Rourke an offer she couldn't refuse.

The brief, yet purposeful encounter terminated as Mr O'Rourke, dressed in trousers, braces and a scruffy vest appeared at the front door.

'We will, we will, Father. Oh yes, we will, Father. Next Sunday we will all be there, Father. All be there.' The reassurances seemed to pour from the Sligo man. His apologetic words dislodged cigarette ash from the roll-up permanently stuck to his top lip. Father Brennan returned to the presbytery, job done.

I would attend mass with my mother and gran. For me it was a duty, a chore. I would be scrubbed senseless by my mother and then put on my Sunday best. We all had to look respectable for God. I hope he showed us the same courtesy. The pagans in our street would watch us go and make polite conversation with us. Comments like,

'Oooh, doesn't he look nice, Nancy?' and 'Who got you ready, chuck?' were well meaning but embarrassing.

Eleven o'clock mass was the most popular service. The majority of the men in the congregation would always sit at the back. At twelve noon, following a much awaited 'Pax Vobiscum' from the priest, they would then hurry across the road to The Grapes.

The hour-long mass was itself a purgatorial experience. Uncomfortable pews and hard kneeling surfaces antagonized the cuts and bruises already on my knees. You would sit down and then a minute later you were up again. Genuflections, Signs of the Cross, rosary beads and Communion bread were the order of the day. Consuming the latter was like trying to swallow a piece of cardboard. Susan Baldock told me you weren't supposed to chew it but slowly let it dissolve in your mouth. If you didn't do this then God would kill you. It stayed there for ages and would refuse to disappear. Its taste was vile. I used to get out my handkerchief and pretend to blow my nose. Underneath the tissue I would chew away at the thing like fury and then swallow, hoping God would spare me.

Two of my mates, Tony Lorenzo and Stefan Podgorski, were altar boys. Tony, a pleasant lad who looked like a diminutive Victor Mature, should never have taken on such a roll. Father Brennan seemed obsessed with incense. He would wave the golden incense burner in a way Genghis Khan would have wielded an axe, filling the altar with sickly smelling smoke. This localized pea souper

would immediately trigger Tony's asthma, leading to him being unceremoniously pushed into the anteroom by Father Brennan, to recover. The rule was simple, no wheezing or dying on the altar.

I first became aware of group narcolepsy during Father Brennan's sermons. Several adults fixed him with an interested stare. Some tried desperately to hold back yawns whilst others experienced the nodding and dribbling side-effects of an induced coma. Even the unyielding nature of the wooden pews would not prevent Mrs Feingold from re-acquainting herself with Morpheus. At the age of nine, even I was puzzled as to why a person with the surname Feingold was regularly asleep inside a Catholic church.

His sermons were both jejune and predictable. As an orator he would have made the boxer Freddie Mills sound like Pericles. His God-fearing message was delivered in an Hibernian drawl which would simmer for ten minutes and then characteristically come to the boil at fifteen. That used to wake them up. Shouts about fire and brimstone, the furnaces of hell and sinners repent provided an alarm call for some and a laxative for others.

They say, 'Hard work never killed anyone.' It certainly killed my gran This lady worked continuously from the age of thirteen until sixty-five. Exposure to the workings of cotton mill machinery for forty years had rendered her quite deaf, as well as suffering from 'cotton lung'. Chronic heart disease eventually terminated her contract.

It was around two o'clock in the morning when my mother woke me.

'Brian, go to the telephone on Broad Street and phone for the doctor. Your gran's not well. Tell him She's having pains in her chest and they're getting worse. I've left the money on the mantelpiece and the number's next to it,' she added.

I quickly dressed, grabbed the pennies and ran as fast as I could to the telephone box near Pendleton Church. Having done battle with buttons A and B, I explained the nature of gran's sickness to the sleepy Doctor Curran.

I was not allowed in to see her in her agony. I just listened as best I could on the landing. My second journey that night was to the presbytery of St James! I rang the doorbell twice and, after what seemed an age, Mrs McNamara the housekeeper opened the door.

I had been rehearsing the message over and over as I ran along Hankinson Street.
    'Can you send a priest to my gran at 7, Strawberry Road? The doctor said she needs the last rites, Mrs McNamara. And me mum says for me to say please.'

The knock on the door heralded a priest's determination to absolve my gran of her sins and to prepare her a future life with God. Again I stood near the foot of the stairs as my mother let him in. It was Father Brennan, dressed in his customary black suit. His dog collar was slightly askew and he was wearing his slippers. Under his arm was a box containing paraphernalia for granting Absolution. Both he and my mother disappeared upstairs where my gran lay dying.

Mrs Tattersall, my mum's friend, sat with me in the parlour.

Half an hour had passed when I heard the bedroom door open. I could hear my mother sobbing. Heavy footsteps down the stairs signalled Father Brennan had done his job. The parlour door then opened and in he came.

I was sitting alongside Mrs Tattersall, who had her arm around my shoulders. I recall my immediate thoughts being, 'Why him? Why not Father Wood? Everyone liked Father Wood. He was young, dynamic and gregarious. Why did it have to be this bloke?' I hated him.

He pulled up a chair and sat immediately opposite me. The events of the night, culminating in the sudden loss of my gran, left me both anxious and confused. To be honest, I wasn't sure how I should be feeling.

'I am very sorry, Brian, but your gran has passed away,' he said, stooped over with his head down. He addressed me in a way I had never heard him speak before. Gone was his sharp and powerful inflection. His voice was soft and gentle. His manner, tender and humble.

'I know you're upset and you're bound to miss her. She was a good woman, Brian. A good, kind woman,' he continued.

'You know, I can understand how you are feeling, son. I lost my mother when I was your age. She was my best friend and I loved her dearly. I bore feelings of emptiness and loneliness for a long time that made me feel bitter towards God. Why did he have to take her from me? Why not take bad people who do wrong? All those thoughts went through my mind, as it will yours.'

He paused and took a deeper breath. It was the quietness and the concern in his voice that took me by surprise.

'She was in a lot of pain you see, Brian. The doctor said he could do no more for her. Now she's at rest you see, son. She's not in any pain now and God is going to look after her for you.' He outstretched his hand and held mine.

'It's an awful thing for you and your mum to have to come to terms with. But you both wouldn't have wanted her to suffer and she's at peace now. I know the grief and sadness both you and your mum will suffer and you must try to be strong for each other. Cry all you want, Brian. It's the right thing to do. I am so, so sorry about your sad loss, son. If you or your mother need to speak to me, if anything is troubling or worrying you, then come and see me any time.'

He again squeezed my hand, then nodded to Mrs Tattersall and rose. He gently closed the door behind him.

Father Wood conducted my gran's funeral, much to the relief of my mates, neighbours and Auntie Cissie, who all shared a mutual dislike for Father Brennan.

'I wouldn't fancy saying cheerio to this world and that heartless bugger seeing me off,' moaned Cissie to Mrs Tattersall.

This time last year I would definitely have agreed with this loud, domineering lady. But now... Do you know? I'm not so sure.

Fancy That?

You could walk past it on a Sunday and not know it was there. Any other day would find you irresistibly drawn to it like sailors to a Siren-clad rock. It was the smell of fresh baked bread, pies, fancies and the unquestionably succulent wimberry tarts. The bouquet that subtly effused from these premises would have instantly made Pavlov's dogs perform. In my opinion, the unpretentious, yet sumptuous wimberry pastry should have been available only on prescription, since a first bite would produce a dependency stronger than any opiate drug. The shop's esteemed meat and potato pies were affectionately referred to as 'growler pies' by the local male population, reflecting the sounds they would make as the pastry was aggressively devoured with a Neanderthal determination.

The small shop in question was Byron's Confectioners, nestled between Ossie Clegg's butchers and Shadrack's haberdashers. The Clegg emporium sold meats of all descriptions from hare to heifer. The proprietor, sporting a striped apron and white cap, had a repetitious catchphrase,
'What's that you want, love? A sheep's head? I'll leave the eyes in so it'll see you through the week!'
His whimsical routine would force the likes of regular customer, Mrs Ivy Sedgewick, to conclude,
'Ossie's a nice chap, but a boring bugger.'

Peggy Shadrack, having been bombed out of her premises in Seedley, had moved into the shop some eight years ago. She would frequently relate to her customers the trauma of such an experience.

'I remember, ladies,' she would say, 'there was this almighty explosion and I came up from the cellar in my nightie. There she was, me mother, stretched out across the kitchen table, pinned down by a heavy pole.'

'Oh, you needn't tell me about that, Peggy,' interrupted Mrs. Winterbottom, 'my mother used to say the Yanks were just as randy!'

Work would begin in the Byron's emporium at 4.30am. George, master baker and former Desert Rat, would have fired the twin-banked ovens on his return from the Conservative Club at 11.30pm the night before. On occasions, following a particularly enjoyable evening and forgetting to prime these furnaces, morning pie sales would be embarrassingly delayed. On windy nights he would attempt to stay awake and ensure the flames didn't blow out and gas everyone.

The business's success was down to his wife, Lottie. She was the skilled patisserie technician, capable of producing the finest of cakes and pastry delicacies. It always seemed fitting that the shop should sell Eccles cakes, being situated on Regent Street, Eccles. The shop window at mid-morning would glow with shelves of a seductive range of custard tarts, maids of honour, cream horns and vanilla slices, all having been freshly prepared on the premises.

At 5am the shop would take its first delivery. The flour men would shoulder two hundred weight sacks of Canadian flour and drop them in the corner of the bakehouse. Each wore a bibbed overall, cotton jacket and cloth cap, all blanched by years of carrying bags of the white stuff. Their gaunt flour-covered faces gave them a supernatural appearance. It was almost as though they had been exhumed hours earlier. Their eeriness was exaggerated by the fact they would say nothing as the sacks were hawked through the shop.

'Eh up, Lottie, Marley's ghosts are here,' George would shout over the noise of the dough mixers, as their wagon drew up outside the shop.

You could set your watch by Walter the milkman. Four crates of full cream milk, tubs of fresh cream and a bottle of sterilized milk was the daily order. Myra, the shop assistant who resembled Popeye's sweetheart, Olive Oyl, would only drink her tea with 'sterra' as she called it. Myra was a loyal worker who looked as though she'd toiled non-stop since the Pleistocene era.

Walter spoke with a broad Salford accent. Words containing a double T would be pronounced with a K. Hence, Walter's attempts at articulating the words 'A little bottle of milk' would translate as 'A likkle bokkle o' milk'. Any conversation from him would be further troubled by a set of ill-fitting dentures that would slip and protrude mid-sentence. Linguistic experts would have diagnosed he had less of an accent and more an impediment.

As a reward for dropping off a couple of extra bokkles, Walter would be given his favourite cheese and onion pie. Now this was worth waiting for. Standing with his back to one of the ovens in an attempt to keep warm, he would then remove the top and bottom set of teeth and stand them on the draining board of the sink. The pie would be slowly sucked into his mouth and then broken up by both tongue and gums.

'Don't go forgetting yer nashers, Watty,' George would say as he moved dough from the prover.

'Oh, they're not mine, George, I'm breaking 'em in for someone else,' quipped Walter as he sprayed the sultana bins with semi-liquid pie.

I attended primary school with George and Lottie's son, David. Our teacher, Miss Morgan, once said of him,

'David always seems to smell like fresh bread'.

He was not a malevolent boy, it was just that he had been given too much time to himself. His parents always seemed to be in the bakehouse or serving customers. In his early years, an attempt to descend into the bakehouse from the small flat above, saw him tumble down the stairs, his fall being broken by a large carton of Corn Flakes. The gradient of the stairway seemed to have the same scale as the north face of the Eiger and required similar mountaineering skills to make a safe descent. On another occasion he accidentally toppled into the huge mixer, with its gyrating paddles capable of scything through all textures of dough. He escaped decapitation but suffered bruising, mild concussion and, as rumour had it, circumcision.

His inquisitive nature was at odds with the health and safety of that time. Unknown to his parents, he would do battle with the pastry pie blockers. These heavy instruments would mould the shape of pies and I was surprised he still possessed a full set of digits.

Having this surplus of unsupervised time on his hands, his inquisitive mind made him experiment. Once, his research into combustion forced him quickly to conclude that Ronson lighter fuel was highly flammable and showed no respect for horse hair sofas and front room curtains. The blaze was subsequently subdued by several buckets of water. George then set about administering a reprimand of a similar magnitude to that he'd last used against the Wehrmacht at Monte Cassino.

I witnessed the pasting he administered. George lifted one of his son's arms and attempted to smack his legs. To avoid the contact of hand against thigh, David would run round his dad, some of the blows missing and others making loud contact. The disciplinary carousel was almost comical to watch. Both parties would suffer as a result of this punishment method, one nursed smarting legs whilst the other recovered from dizziness. George, indeed, had a fiery temper aggravated by never having enough hours in the day to get things done.

The local kids would often use Eccles churchyard for playing Japs and commandos. Their ungracious use of the grimy Victorian gravestones gave plenty of cover as they lobbed pretend hand grenades at each other. They coupled this with shooting deadly sprays of machine gun fire.

'DAKKA, DAKKA, DAKKA!' would rip from their vocal cords as they leapt from the grave of factory worker to factory owner. The more opulent the corpse, the bigger the headstone but the better was the camouflage.

The one thing that got on everyone's nerves was that during any skirmish, Laurence Epstein would never be killed. You could stand there in front of him, having already blown him up with a Molotov cocktail and DAKKA, DAKKA him 'til sunset. He would still refuse to drop. In retrospect I suppose he regarded it as good training for his future role in defending the Golan Heights.

It was following a re-enactment of the Malaya conflict that the discovery was made. The rest of the gang were now on their way home, moaning about Laurence and sympathising with Kenny Bostock for losing his dad's Burma Star medal, all commiserating with the impending thrashing he would receive.

The thought of returning home and being made to fold cardboard cake boxes was of little appeal to David. A desire to build an improved defensive

position for tomorrow's battle presented greater appeal. It was during his excavations that he discovered a metal tube about the size of a twelve-inch ruler sticking out of the ground close to the graveyard wall. Some preliminary clearance and a few final tugs saw its exhumation complete. He picked up the grey cylinder, covered in clods of clay, and took it home.

The shop was unusually full for a Thursday afternoon. People were obviously stocking up for the impending bank holiday weekend. The customers merrily exchanged tittle-tattle,

'An' I'll tell you this, Lottie, she's no better than she ought to be,' whispered Mrs. Littlewood as she leaned over the counter.

'Oh, and I'll take a box of fancies, if I may?' she continued.

The door to the shop was open and Lottie's grubby and war-torn eight-year-old quickly side-stepped between the gossiping customers. Most of them were too busy to acknowledge him but finally Mrs Eckersley, a portly woman with a repartee better than Max Miller, detected the young lad's presence and cried,

'Here he is, Lottie! Here's yer little 'un. What's that you got, love?'

There was a momentary pause when a shaft of alarm terminated the pleasantries.

'Jeeeeesus Chrrrrist almighty! The little bugger's got a bomb!'

This was indeed a horrifying yet accurate analysis of the situation in that the boy was carrying an incendiary bomb; a present from The Luftwaffe following their attempt in 1940 to flatten Trafford Park. It was an outburst that brought panic and hysteria to the small Eccles shop. The corpulent Mrs Eckersley arrived at the shop door at the same time as another equally proportioned customer. The two acted like a volcanic plug sealing the exit for others equally as desperate to vacate the premises. After three strategically placed lunges, Miss Bottomley cleared the obstruction with her umbrella. The shop emptied with the speed of a moonlight flit.

'Geeoooooorge! Geeoooooorge!' bawled Lottie. 'Our David's got an incendiary bomb!'

At this moment George was murdering a Players Navy Cut at the back of the bakery and the cry for help coincided with his crescendo of smoke inhalation. He ran through the bakehouse coughing and spluttering and on entering the shop, grabbed hold of the rather bewildered child who

was currently attempting to twist the fins of the device.

'Go and get Ossie Clegg, Lottie, and ask him for his stirrup pump,' bellowed George as he picked up both boy and bomb and charged out into the back yard. He snatched the explosive from the child's tiny fingers and placed it in a fire bucket that until now had only been used for cigarette ends.

'Gerrup those stairs and gerrin yer bedroom, you stupid kid!'

You did what George said at times like these, particularly when he punctuated his sentences with a slap.

'What the 'ell's the matter, George?' called Ossie as he entered the yard through the back gate. He carried a bucket of water and an old ARP stirrup pump.

'Oh, blood and sand, George, where did you get that?' he worryingly inquired.

'Our David dug it up. The lad's cracked, Ossie, I tell you, he's ruddy well tapped,' wheezed George, who was now squirting water at the half-submerged bomb canister.

Lottie rushed into the yard from the bakehouse and joined the butcher and the baker. Unfortunately there was no candlestick maker to complete the nursery rhyme.

'I've told Myra to get the police and I wouldn't bother with that old thing,' said the breathless Lottie, pointing to the special issue stirrup pump.

'They're about as useful as a chocolate fireguard.'

The police called the fire brigade, who then rang the army ordnance. An ambulance arrived, though no-one admitted contacting them. The incendiary device was safely removed and details of the afternoon's excitement made page two of the Eccles and Patricroft Journal.

A pair of tearful eyes gazed down from the bedroom window whilst men in uniform took control of the situation. He hadn't meant to cause all of this fuss. He didn't know it was a bomb. He didn't know he could have blown himself up and torched half of Eccles. All he did know was he was going to get it from his dad.

A shout of, 'David? David?' cracked through the air as George noisily climbed the stairs. Such thunder and determination seemed to rubber stamp an imminent yet familiar thrashing carousel.
   Happy days?

Please, Miss?

I had been taken to this strange place once before, but only for an afternoon. Now my mother was bringing me here again but at 8.30 in the morning. She pushed open a squeaky metal gate showing signs of rust and chipped paint. The gate had a sliding latch attached to which was a huge padlock. Most mums found this bar hard to move sideways and gain access to the tarmaced area immediately in front of the grey, unwelcoming, Victorian building.

I was holding my mum's hand as we crossed this open space and I became aware that my grip on her fingers was becoming even tighter the more we advanced towards a large semi-glazed wooden door. This heavy structure marked the entrance to the building. Several other little boys and girls, also accompanied by their mums, were taking a similar route. One miserable soul was crying and pushing his feet hard against the pavement refusing to move. Another child was screaming to his embarrassed mother that he didn't want to go and struck out at her arms with his navy plimsoll bag. Such antagonism and misery did me no good at all. I choked back my tears and reluctantly followed my mother.

The doorknob of this awkward, emerald green portal was a large polished brass sphere that needed twisting and pulling hard. It was too high for me, and anyway, I didn't really want to co-operate with any means of entering this place. I could sense some life-changing experience was in store for me.

Once inside we negotiated a corridor bustling and resonating with the sounds of children. The noise was overpowering and hurt my ears. Rows of coat pegs projected angrily from the walls, one large spike with a smaller one below, festooned with coats, scarves, mittens and PE bags all dangling and being buffeted by passers-by. The passageway had windows along one side and on the wall opposite were displays showing infantile creative work in *papier mache*, poster paint, raffia and wool.

Room 1A, situated behind the third door on the right, was our destination. Its space was filled with four rows of metal framed desks at which were seated some anxious children with despondent faces. The last time I witnessed such melancholy and tension was in Mr Price, the dentist's waiting room. Saying goodbye to my mother made me the loneliest person on the planet. Our parting was an *au revoir* rather than a permanent separation and there was a promise of a bottle of Vimto and a sherbet dip when she returned. The hand bell being rung at 3.45pm seemed years away. Such parting induced a feeling inside me of emptiness and heartbreak, the likes of which I had sensed only once before when our dog, Rex, was electrocuted by chewing through the flex of the electric iron. Today marked my initial sortie into the world of compulsory education and a seven-year sentence at John Street Primary School.

Our teacher for this introductory year was Miss Lewis, a portly young lady and as I overheard one parent describe her,
   'Aye, she's a fair faced lass, but it's a pity about her titty bottle legs.'

Her morphology did improve the further up her body you travelled. She had a rounded face with high cheekbones and she wore just the minimum amount of make-up to highlight her appealing features. Her eyes were an azure blue, and her hair was always neatly tied into a tight bun. Miss Lewis seemed to be constantly tying our shoelaces and buttoning our coats. Zips continued to be a mystery to us all until the age of six. She was the youngest teacher in the school and at that point in time we didn't realize how fortunate we were to receive her constant attention.

In a year's time our class would discover that being educated by another teacher, Miss Newton, was like being supervised by an active member of the Waffen SS, and you certainly did as you were told. Miss Newton reminded us of a witch. She had a lump on the end of her pointed chin and her gnarled face never changed in its expression. It was as though she was constantly sucking a piece of lemon. She wore a kilt, fastened at its base by a huge safety pin, and a chunky Fair Isle jumper even on a warm summer's day. Her frumpy shoes reflected her no-nonsense manner. Mums would describe this footwear as 'sensible', however, the children in years to come would have labelled them as 'assertive and confrontational'. As opposed to Miss Lewis, she wore no make-up whatsoever and any facial rouge she sometimes acquired was due to transient bouts of blood pressure.

Miss Newton's teaching methodology was based on the law of the conservation of energy as she remained seated at her desk for the whole day. When she had to administer frequent corporal punishment to classroom felons, she would instruct them to stand on a chair next to her desk and then smack them hard on the back of their legs.

The majority of primary schools at this time showed a gender bias among its teaching staff. Mr Skinner, the Head Teacher, was the only male teacher in this establishment; even the caretaker, Mrs Fishwick, was female (rumour had it). 'Lenny', as the older boys and girls would call Mr Skinner, had escaped duties with the armed services during the '39-'45 conflict because of fallen arches and, as we suspected, innate cowardice. He was a very tall, skinny chap with a nose that can only be likened to a blind cobbler's thumb. Ivor Culshaw's mother reckoned that if he had enlisted, the sight of his terrifying proboscis would have forced the Bosch back across the Rhine two years earlier. He too wore the same clothes each day and his shiny double-breasted pinstriped suit trousers bore flecks of chewing gum and ink blotches on their rear. His starched shirt collar displayed a blue tie encrusted with egg yolk and marmalade.

Mr Skinner spoke with a broad Salford accent and used the English language like a Rubik's cube. He was a man with letters behind his name that had been donated by a pupil Cyril Delaney, as a result of him being publicly flogged by Skinner in front of the whole school. At the age of five I had never encountered such a qualification acronym. At the age of fifteen, however, the letters on the wooden school sign spelt a very rude word. Everyone, even Mrs Skinner, was terrified of him. He displayed the warmth and sensitivity of Dr. Josef Mengele, yet he was idolised by his concubine, Miss Newton.

My class contained the predictable mix of 'characters'. There was the ever-silent Barry

Dobson, whose catatonic behaviour forced other five-year-olds to think of him as weird. The only noise that came from him were burps. Terry Brady was constantly itching and I never enjoyed him sitting nearby. Angus Choudhury, a very bright boy, was to be of use to us all in future years by allowing classmates to copy his maths homework. Angus's parents met during the war. His mother was from Paisley and his dad, a loyal colonialist who joined the Lancashire Fusiliers, was from the Punjab. Stefan Jaswinski was always happy even if something serious had occurred, like losing his dinner money. His cheerful nature helped all of us cope with those infant years but sadly he succumbed to polio and died by the age of eight. Indeed, there were many sickly children in the school suffering from a variety of ailments, from chronic bronchitis to malnutrition. Thank heavens for free school milk and orange juice. To complete the health picture, very few of us escaped nits and the fine toothcomb and newspaper came out three or four times a year.

The girls in our class varied as much as the boys. Sheila Dennis was the supergrass of the group and took pleasure informing the teachers of unacceptable behaviour, usually from the boys. Her quisling nature made her the ideal choice for classroom monitor, and rumour had it that she even 'shopped' her brother, Philip, when he stole the vinegar bottle from Kirby's chip shop. Incidentally, the sign above this gastronomic emporium read:
   'Kirby's Chipy'
   'The Best Cod and Hadock in the North West'

Harry Kirby would, indeed, have benefited from today's literacy hour.

Beverley Battersby was a superb gymnast. She would push her school skirt into her navy blue knickers and perform handstands with ease against the school wall. Hopscotch too would be completed at supersonic speeds. Her co-ordination was undisputed, for she was the only person in the school who could juggle four tennis balls at once. Most girls could barely manage two as they chanted,

'One O'Leary, two O'Leary, three O'Leary, four.'

Elaine Duxbury's hair was always neatly done in pigtails and each day her shiny auburn locks would develop deep blue tips as boys seated behind her, dipped them in two ink wells.

The first year at John Street School was, as far as I can remember, an enjoyable one. We all looked forward to storytime and Miss Lewis told us yarns that had us spellbound, so much so that Horace Duckinfield would wet himself rather than miss the end of the story. Tales of sailors travelling to faraway lands, teddy bears that could talk, and giants who were frightened of mice, all brought Mrs Fishwick, the school caretaker, and her mop and bucket to classroom 1A. Indeed, her daytime janitorial duties mostly involved her carrying this or a bucket of sand to absorb patches of sick.

Mrs Fishwick, known to the older boys and girls as 'Mrs Fishface', took great pride in her toilets, as she referred to them. These outside buildings were freezing cold even during the summer term. Cracked wooden seats that on occasion nipped the skin on your bottom, were partnered with Izal toilet paper dispensers. This stuff may well have medicated your hands when you wiped your bottom, but unfortunately it had the absorbency of a roof tile and just moved around what you were wiping. When the school ran out of toilet paper, torn up squares of the *Daily Sketch* or *Daily Express* came off the subs bench. It was like being at home. There was one toilet cubicle that was reserved for us 'little uns'. It had a stone step up to the WC for girls to access the seat and for boys to be able to aim inside the bowl, which few of them managed.

Older children looked so big, and we were often knocked over by them in the playground as they played their energetic games. Should you be flattened by a ten-year-old, they were usually very apologetic and picked you up and dusted you down. If the trauma of you being made supine caused you to cry, they would help dry your eyes with a section of your pullover before being admonished for causing your tears by a passing dinner lady. A small, caged playground on the roof of the building was reserved for the more senior members of the school community to avoid some of these play area collisions.

I was amazed at the number of games that could be played in such a confined area. Eight-year-old boys would tear around the playground playing football. Goalposts were a pile of coats dropped strategically on the playground, or alternatively there were chalked marks on a wall. Others would play cowboys and Indians, galloping across the play area and slapping their thighs to make their imaginary horses go faster. Girls would play 'twosies' against a high walled part of the building. Some chose skipping or less energetic guessing games. A favourite one was 'I draw a snake upon your back and guess who tigged it'. This involved a group of girls standing behind somebody who was facing a wall. They would all draw a snake-like line on the person's back with their fingers and one of them would administer a final dot (tig them). The girl who was tigged then had to guess the tigger. Not exactly MENSA stuff, I know, but everyone seemed to be entertained. It was always easy to know when the gargantuan and extremely inept Doreen McClaggen tigged you, since the bruising you received remained painful for weeks.

The first fun I had in the autumn term of my new school life was playing conkers. My uncle John had to pierce them with a meat skewer for me after I nearly achieved human brochette status trying this operation. Someone told me to soak the conkers in vinegar or paint them with clear nail varnish to toughen their surface. This recipe met with limited success. Conkers would be graded as to the number of contests they had won. Twoers, threeers and, the most rare, fourers all appeared battle fatigued and eventually would split, throwing horse chestnut shrapnel in all directions. I was the worst conker player ever, though slightly better than Leslie Arnison, who was responsible for more contused knuckles than a heavyweight boxer. Receiving a blow across your fingers from one of his conkers on a cold October morning was a painful experience.

Once a week, during morning registration, Miss Lewis would collect dinner money. This was brought to school in a paper bag or an envelope, tightly folded so that girls could roll it inside their knickers. Boys frequently dropped their bag of money in the playground and the mixture of silver, threepenny bits and copper would roll off in all directions. Many of us were on free school meals and I always thought it rather humiliating that these dinner tickets were a different colour. Such disparity inevitably gave rise to intrusive questions like:

'Why have you got a yellow ticket and I've got a green one?'

'Where's your dinner money? You never hand it in.'

'Are you poor then?'

School dinners at John Street School were not cooked on the premises. Instead they were shipped in, having been prepared at the council kitchens. I remember the clatter and crashing sounds as the delivery-men heaved large stainless steel canisters and tins into the school hall. Each item had lids held in place by a pair of clasps. At lunchtime us babies were allowed in first, in order to avoid being crushed by older children. There was always a shortage of cutlery and the practice was to spit on your knife, fork and spoon as soon as you picked them out of the tray. This would deter older kids stealing them from you.

The lunches, served up by a most ferocious coven of dinner ladies, were splotched onto your plate then off you went to the dinner tables. The weekly shepherd's pie was perseveringly chewed as though the shepherd, complete with his wellies, was in it. In fact, I'm still chomping bits of it to this day.

'Does anyone want me swede?' enquired an unhappy Vernon Midgley.

'While you are at it, does anyone want me semolina as well?' he continued.

Patrick O'Driscoll would eat anything, from woody root vegetables to stringy cabbage. Most of our class offloaded any inedible components to him and Miss Lewis would subsequently have to ask him to visit the toilet during afternoon school. I believe Patrick to be the initial cause of global warming.

School assemblies took place each morning after registration. Each year cohort would pile into the small hall and we would sit on the cold linoleum floor. There was a piano in the corner of the room at which Mrs Goodbody would be seated on special days. Her niche was to accompany our singing. It was tragic irony that a lady with the name Goodbody should be so largely proportioned that she seemed to absorb the piano stool, and from a distance she looked seated on a single pole. What had she done with the rest of the seat? She played this instrument as though she was frightened of it rolling away from her. Hence, she would punch the piano keys with her courgette-like fingers, and the harmonics emanating from the said machine would rattle the glass windows.

A typical assembly would include a story, usually from the Bible. This story always had a moral that not many of us little ones understood. On occasions there was a 'show me' slot whereby some clever clogs, having invented something or created a model of Blackpool Tower using hair grips, was asked to show it to the school. Commendations were issued to the assiduous members of our pupil fraternity and 'tellings off' were administered to the naughty element of this same brotherhood. Mr Skinner usually conducted proceedings and we all wondered what he did for the rest of the day.

My induction year in Miss Lewis's class included playing with sand, water, plasticine, white glue, crayons, raffia and paints. Coloured card was cut badly with impossible scissors, and tissue paper was fashioned into all sorts of objects. There was, however, an emphasis more on learning than on play. We were introduced to those terribly painful things such as tables, spellings and writing. There was a powerful emphasis on the 3Rs. Little did we know that these embryo learning years would culminate in that eleven plus exam, whose results would often break up friendship groups.

My first day at John Street School finished with the same unhappiness as it had started. Miss Lewis had allowed me to go to the toilet before her end of day story. I was walking back across the yard looking at the gate at which my mother would soon appear, complete with a bottle of 'pop' and sweeties. I suddenly looked down to see the heel of my shoe hanging off. I wasn't too sure of how to solve this problem and as I stood looking at the offending footwear, an older boy from the juniors walked by.

'Do you want your shoe mended?' he said in a patronizing voice.

'Yes, please,' I replied, thankful that someone was prepared to help me.

'Go over to that room over there. Knock on the door and say to the tall bloke inside, that you'd like him to mend your shoe,' the pupil advised.

He steered me in the direction of a large battleship grey door and as I was just about to knock, the door opened. There stood the tall figure of Mr Skinner, who stooped over me like a vulture about to rip apart its prey.

'Can you mend me shoe please?' I timidly enquired.

I felt his arm come down on my shoulder and raise me up in the air. He held me at his eye level with my feet dangling. I don't think I had experienced such an altitude before.

'Can I mend your shoe?' he bawled. 'Can I mend your shoe?' he repeated at an even louder volume. Although I had just visited the toilet, I mysteriously found some extra wee from somewhere and became conscious of wet underpants.

'Get back to your class and stop wasting my time,' he yelled as he returned me to terra firma.

'Leave the lad alone, he's only a likkle 'un!' boomed Mrs Doherty from behind the school gates. Mrs Mavis Doherty was a parent, born and bred in Hanky Park, whose son was in the top juniors. This lady, like most females from this district, called a spade a spade until she tripped over one. She had an acerbic tongue and she let fly at him with some choice vocabulary.

Mr Skinner's answer to her fiery rhetoric came as he turned towards her and took a few paces forward.

'Madam!' he boomed in a deep bellicose voice, desperately trying to maintain an air of superiority. 'I am paid for what I know!' he continued.

'Well, ya can't be paid that bleedin' much then!' responded the quick- witted Mrs Doherty. Her sharp assault on Mr Skinner's credibility forced him to turn away and make no further response.

I ached for home time and the sound of Julie Redman ringing the school bell. Julie was a top junior

who tackled her role of bell monitor with such gusto she would have deafened the likes of Quasimodo. If this was school then I didn't want to know. Well... maybe a prescription bottle of Vimto, a penny Spanish and a sherbet dip would provide a remedy to ease my trauma. Indeed, the daily dose of such toothsome pharmacy seemed to get me through that first term at John Street Primary School.

Five Park Drive

It had been a particularly bad week. I had been looking forward to half term and playing out with my mates. Bogey racing (primitive go-karts using pram wheels and a plank of wood) and football were on the menu for the boys whilst skipping, with a huge lorry rope with one end tied to the lamppost, was for the girls.

I always thought the girls were remarkably brave to even attempt this activity since the rope was incredibly heavy and took three of them, with the exception of 'big' Edna Jackson, to turn it. Edna's soubriquet 'big', was an obvious choice for she would have dwarfed St Helen's rugby league star Vince Karalius.

Should you be caught and struck by this rope as it rotated at speed, the blow could induce contusions and even coma. I once saw Henry Burke attempt to go 'under the moon and over the stars', the circling rope simulating both celestial components. He went under the rope with ease, even Kevin Tooley could do that and he was the most uncoordinated person I have seen. Leaping over the rope was another matter and took some concentration. Henry was clearly preoccupied hearing that United were two nil down to Luton Town, and his assault on the contraption proved almost fatal. The rope strangled him just as he was emerging from the other side. His neck remained bruised and swollen for weeks. My mum said he looked as though he had been a victim of garrotting by the Mafia.

Any optimism I had for the week was quickly blighted when my gran had one of her 'funny turns'. I never could find this term in any dictionary but my take on this nebulous debility was that, should an old person suffer from this medical condition, they must sit in an armchair all day and issue orders to children. As a result of this mysterious disease, her symptoms caused me to miss most of the half-term activities I had been looking forward to.

Day one of her malady saw me paying the coalman for dropping two bags of nutty slack down our coal-hole and then sweeping up after them. The coal came on a cart pulled by a mangy-looking horse wearing blinkers. The coalmen looked equally as mangy but took on the appearance of two George Mitchell Black and White Minstrels, their faces smudged and blackened with coal dust. They wore tatty leather jackets that looked a couple of sizes too big for them and a cap with a leather neckguard. They really were a slatternly duo.

My next duty also involved coal husbandry. Down the cellar I would go, armed with a hammer to break up the large pieces of coal into smaller, more combustible fragments. I hated the cellar because it terrified me. There was no electricity down there. You had to light a candle and this would feebly illuminate cobwebs and silhouette strange and eerie shapes. My appetite for Dickens' novels and my outrageous imagination allowed me to expect the likes of Miss Havisham or Abel Magwitch to be hiding down there.

Another duty was to run endless errands for her. My gran would shout,

'Don't forget to get me divvy at the Co-op and I'll have a bag of sugar and a quarter o' tea. Your mother brought home some o' that Camp Coffee t' other day. God, I thought she was trying to poison me. Tasted like liquid horse manure, I tell you!'

Of course, the rationale behind such an accusation meant that at some stage in her life she had at least sipped liquid horse manure. Perhaps this could precipitate 'funny turns' later in life?

Twice a week she would have a bet. I was the one charged with the responsibility of putting on the wager. The local back-street bookie was a spivvish character, known to his punters as Mickey Finn. He plied his trade at the rear of a large end-of-terrace house at the top of Hankinson Street. I never went in. A hard knock on the back yard door and a face would appear at a tiny hatch.

'What do ya want, kid?' growled the face with a roll-up and halitosis.

'I've got a bet here for Nan Number 7. Sixpence each way on Tornado, 3.15 at Kempton.'

'Give us it here,' he muttered.

I handed the note and money through the hatch and waited a few moments. He returned and gave me a docket, thus registering the bet. A couple of older boys pushed past me and entered the house. They were in Mickey Finn's employment and acted as bookie's runners, relaying bets from the men in the factories nearby.

Tornado indeed! My gran never had any luck on the horses. Tornado turned out to be more like a gentle breeze and never finished a race.

The curious irony of Mickey's illicit back street profession was that his premises were situated across the road from Pendleton police station.

I had no sooner returned from this errand than another was put my way. It was the customary visit to Henshaw's Pawnbrokers to generate a little revenue until my mother was paid on Friday.

'Don't tell me. Is it the wedding ring or the watch?'

Mr Henshaw sat on a high chair behind the counter and would gaze down upon his customers over his pince-nez spectacles. I frequently observed him rummaging through pawned bedding, armed with a pin to stab any bed bugs caught up in the material.

'It's the watch, Mr Henshaw. Me gran says can you do the same as last time?' I nervously inquired.

'Two pound. Take it or leave it,' came his brusque response.

'Aye, ok then. Ta.'

I handed over my grandad's pocket watch, collected the ticket and the two pound notes. The rapid fiscal transaction and his reluctance to bargain made me recall my gran's summary of the man.

'He's as tight as a duck's bum in water. He wouldn't give you the drips off the end of his nose.'

This was quite a graphic, yet accurate curriculum vitae of the man I thought. Rumour had it that he allowed his wife to purchase just one box of OMO washing powder per year to meet their laundry needs.

The early part of the evening would see her attempt to remedy her 'funny turns'. She self-prescribed a pharmaceutical cocktail of nicotine and Wilson's bitter.

Five Park Drive and a jug of ale was her usual dosage, and once more I was dispatched to collect the medication from the off-licence of The Bridge public house. This section of the establishment was a small cubicle capable of holding up to three customers, though only one if big Edna Jackson's mum wanted a milk stout. She was even bigger than big Edna herself.

Access to the bar was via a sash window of frosted glass. It was positioned high up in the wall and I had to jump up to tap on it with a half-crown coin.

Vernon the landlord usually dealt with the off-licence clientele. Up came the window and Vernon's face would peer down at me. My Auntie Cissie described Vernon as having a lived-in face. The occupants of his visage were predominantly blackheads and an itinerant boil. Vernon now managed the pub on his own. His wife, deeply affected by Celia Johnson's role in 'Brief Encounter', had been taking advantage of too many 'special offers' from Ted Cardwell, the Smith's Crisps rep and Vernon decided they should part on mutual terms.

'Mutual terms?' Cissie would say. 'He told her to bugger off and she did. Those were the mutual terms.'

'The usual, lad?' he enquired.

'Yes please, Vernon. Five Park Drive and the jug, please?' I replied.

My gran would never drink 'mild'. She always said they (the bar staff) would tip the slops into the mild and so you never knew what you were drinking.

I was fascinated by the interior of The Bridge. If I jumped up and hung onto the small counter, I could see inside. To the right was The Vault or Tap Room. This was where the men drank and smoked. They all looked cloned, each wearing a shabby suit, cloth cap and muffler. I would always see my friend Herbie's dad in there.

'All reet, lad?' he would shout as he saw my face at the window. You could tell when he'd had one too many, which incidentally was most evenings. He would raise his pint, belch and then bring the glass to his lips in an unusual way, seeming to

outline an imaginary circle. It was a miracle he found his mouth with the amount of swaying he did.

To the left was the lounge bar. This was not much different from The Vault in many ways. The linoleum was a lighter colour and there were some shabby upholstered seats. A piano in the corner was for Saturdays and bank holidays. The lounge was where women would drink. Few were with their husbands on weekdays. The men preferred to drink in the Tap Room, seeking conversation about football and sex. On a Saturday night it was different. Couples would dress up in their best clothes and sit together in the lounge singing along to Tommy Polson, who tickled the ivories. I would often lie in bed on a Saturday evening listening to them, accompanied by a man who played the piano with eight digits. Auntie Cissie told my mother that Tommy was a rainproof cutter at Mandelberg's and lost two fingers running some gaberdine through a band saw. Consequently most of the melodies he thrashed out were short of a crotchet or two.

The singing was predictably appalling. Madge Pickup's voice was always fuelled by a plethora of port and lemons. Tommy gave her the apocryphal billing of 'The Pendleton Linnet'. Her ditties were often discordant and bawdy. Her voice gave you tinnitus and the number of words of the song she forgot was directly proportional to her degree of inebriation.

Some of the men's attempts at song were equally frightening. Many pronounced words differently as they shouted into the cheap microphone.

'Hand whhhen hhyew, see the blhue skies hup habove!'

Such renditions posed Mario Lanza's current chart-topping number little threat.

'Goodnight, luv. Safe journey home!'

'Yeh. Mind how ya go. See ya, luv.' Kiss. Kiss.

This kind of drunken bonhomie was clearly audible at chucking out time from couples living only a few doors apart. Their Saturday evening's pleasure would most likely conclude with a bit of 'How's your father?' followed by alcohol-induced slumber.

I thought bitter tasted vile. How grown-ups could pour pints of the stuff down them was beyond me? I would often sip some of the beer through its head as I carefully transported the enamelled jug and the cigarettes home to see if its taste had improved. Maybe mild would be less harsh on the tastebuds?

'Here's your change, gran. Oh, and Herbie's dad asked to be remembered to you,' I said, putting the jug down on the small table next to her seat.

'It's a wonder that bloke can remember anything, the amount of ale he sups,' came her sarcastic riposte.

'Now, go and fill t' coal skuttle and then go and put the candle next t' cistern in t' toilet so it doesn't freeze up,' she ordered.

She knew I hated that job. I would sooner let the outside toilet freeze and then smash the ice with a hammer in the morning.

She had been at me all day. Do this. Do that. I was really annoyed with her incessant demands. I had already missed a game of football and playing 'Robber's Knock' with my mates, seeing to her needs.

I don't know why I did this? Whether it was to pay her back for persecuting me or just to remind her I had a life of my own? I'm not sure. I took one of her Park Drive cigarettes and pushed two rolled up percussion caps, from my Alan Ladd cowboy cap gun, about a quarter of the way into the cigarette. If you completed the insertion with a pin, you couldn't detect their presence.

'Give us one o' me cigs, our Brian,' was a frequent command for which I hadn't long to wait.

She took the loaded cigarette, lit it and drew a lungful of tobacco smoke... Nothing. I sat near the kitchen door waiting for the next inhalation. It came but again... nothing. Had I given her the wrong one? Was there something wrong with the gunpowder?

It was midway through the third drag that she got her come-uppance.

*!*BANG*!* A real loud bang an' all!

I saw it explode and toss half of the cigarette shrapnel into her hairnet. The remaining butt end of the smouldering object hung from her lips. Her eyes wide open, her eyebrows singed. She froze.

'Oh my God, I've killed her,' I said to myself as I watched her rapidly turn grey. She wasn't moving.

'Oh my God, you've killed her,' was my mother's similar diagnosis as she ran in from the parlour.

'Oh my God, you nearly killed me!' came another confirmation, but this time from the lady I'd just killed.

The cigarette stub, still stuck to her upper lip, resembled an exploded spring interior mattress. Her complexion remained an ashen shade.

'Ya stupid, stupid boy. My heart stopped. You could have ruddy well killed me!' bellowed the short-term cadaver.

I knew what was coming next and it hurt. My gran took a swing at me but missed, her lunge weakened by the recent combustion trauma. My mother's swipe connected though, three times. My legs stung and smarted from the blows. Curse short trousers!

There was a knock at the front door.

'Can your Brian come out to play yet?' my mate Herbie politely enquired.

'No he can't, Herbie! Not now or for the rest of the holiday either! He's been a bad lad! A bad, bad lad,' she shouted and slammed the door so hard it made my gran turn grey again.

Well then, so much for half-term?

Mr Price's Drill

It started as a niggle and then, over a period of a fortnight, it became quite troublesome. Looking at the thing in the kitchen mirror, I discovered a small hole that I would eventually stuff with chewing gum, cotton wool soaked in oil of cloves and even TCP in a desperate attempt to stop it aching. Aspirin and whisky lavages were also both self-prescribed and administered, but sadly the pain refused to go away.

It was toothache but on the grand scale. Agonizing pain gave me sleepless nights and miserable days. My lower jaw throbbed on occasions and excruciating shafts of pain darted towards my ear. At times the right side of my head seemed to feel an unrelenting pounding and soreness. I had to let the dentist do his worst.

Mr Price had his practice on Broad Street, an end-of-terrace, accessed by some steep steps. The front window of his surgery was semi-opaque and the lower section bore the sign:
Dental Surgery

V.R. Price BDS (Lond.)
On the wall beneath this notice, some unhappy victim of Mr Price's handiwork had chalked the unflattering words... KILLER.

Victor Price must have qualified in dentistry at the same time as trephination of skulls to release evil vapours was a popular remedy among medics. He seemed ancient to us ten-year-olds. His surgery contained the same instruments of torture he had first purchased on graduating from dental school some forty years earlier. Mr Price had a face that looked uncomfortable with life. His bald pate and wrinkled jowls were partially occluded by a thick pair of black, round-framed spectacles. Seeing him from a distance, which incidentally was the correct place to view him for most people, he resembled a white-coated welder complete with goggles. He possessed, what people would call in those days, a Draught Bass nose that would keep you mesmerized during a check-up. It was also something you wanted to punch when you experienced one of his painful fillings.

Mr Price was a heavy smoker. His fingers appeared ginger and you could smell the Golden Virginia on them as he clumsily poked probes and forceps into your mouth. His unconvincing attempts at bonhomie, only paralleled by Cesare Borgia, doused you with a miasma of stale tobacco breath more potent than his cylinders of anaesthetic gas.

'You'll have to go. I'll make you an appointment on my way to work,' said my mother. 'If you leave that any longer it'll get an abscess on it and then where will you be?' she continued. She'd often used that expression before, 'and then where will you be?' We hadn't the money to go on holiday to Blackpool. We weren't going anywhere and so, in answer to her question, I would still be here.

'Call in at the shop and I'll tell you the time of your appointment. I'll tell him it's an emergency, and mind you go. I don't want you coming home telling me that he wasn't in. And, don't do what Lenny Cardwell did... knocking on the door with a sponge indeed, and telling his mum that nobody answered to let him in. I don't know, some kids think parents are as daft as a brush!'

My appointment was for half past three. The tooth had been unpleasantly painful during the morning, but strangely my discomfort seemed to ease at the beginning of the afternoon. Maybe it was getting better? Should I leave it for a couple more days to see how it goes? Perhaps a bad toothache follows this course – unbearable, leading to milder, more tolerable symptoms? These thoughts almost persuaded me to forfeit my 3.30pm rendezvous. However, a sudden blast of cold air played across the premolar in question as I breathed in, and caused an excruciating shaft of pain to pierce the side of my head. This instant agony reaffirmed my need to consult Mr Price.

Mrs Ida Makepeace doubled as receptionist and dental nurse. Her latter role was simply to hold your head still as her boss, Mr Price, either drilled or pulled your tooth. It must have taken years of training to undertake this technical duty for she had a grip like a professional wrestler. Once she got you in a head-lock, you just couldn't get out of the chair.

I checked in by ringing the front door bell and she came out of the treatment room, put a tick by my name and told me to sit down in the waiting room. The floor of this room was covered in a chequerboard of green and black linoleum. The bareness of the room did nothing for its acoustics. Any sounds emanating from Mr Price's labour would amplify and collect in this waiting area. There were two posters on the shabby wallpaper,

both designed to take a patient's mind away from impending torture. The first was a National Health Service propaganda submission encouraging you to drink more milk and the other, penned by the dental supremo himself, advised you of surgery opening times and not to smoke in the waiting room. That was rich coming from him. People would say he'd drag on a roll-up to calm himself down before he pulled your tooth out. The room boasted eight wooden chairs and a tatty two-seater Chesterfield sofa. I'd seen better quality furniture out on the pavement of the impoverished Ellor Street when families were being evicted.

Looking around the room, I saw two other people awaiting treatment. One was an old chap who persistently let his tongue play around with his dentures, allowing them to protrude from his mouth and then suddenly retract them as fast as a lizard would catch a fly. I recognized the other patient. It was Albie Crump, younger brother of Royston Crump. The family were Lissadel Street residents though Royston seemed to reside more in Strangeways Prison than in the family home. Albie was there with his mum. He had a scarf tied on his head, knotted at the top, which held in place a pad of material designed to keep an aching tooth warm.

I nodded to Albie who painfully returned the acknowledgement, but then the door of the treatment room opened and out came a middle-aged man holding a ball of cotton wool against the corner of his mouth. The material was stained bright red with fresh blood.

'So, I can have a drink tonight then?' the man nervously enquired as he quickly left the room.

'Aye. But wait 'til it congeals though. It was a big un that one,' shouted Mrs Makepeace. The man then hurriedly left the surgery, seeming relieved to be away from the place.

'Have you brought yer teeth with yer, Mr Sexton?' boomed Ida. 'I've got to shout love 'cos he's deaf,' she assured Mrs Crump. 'Just pop 'em in this bag, love, and we'll have 'em ready for yer on Friday. That's it. They'll fit yer better then,' she continued. The old man did as instructed and top and bottom set dropped straight from his mouth into a brown paper bag.

'Right, are you the 3.30?' called Mrs Makepeace as she looked in my direction.

'Er, it's alright Albie, you can go first if you want?' I said. Albie clung even closer to his mother as I made this suggestion.

'It's alright, love, we're not 'til ten to four; you go first,' replied Mrs Crump.

I got up from my chair. My heart was pounding but my tooth wasn't hurting any more. Nevertheless, I walked as dejectedly as a condemned Venetian would have crossed the Bridge of Sighs. The treatment room stank of organic liquids and anaesthetic. The centrepiece of this chamber was the dentist's chair. Nothing about this item of furniture looked welcoming. The chair felt hard. It had a minimum amount of padding and leather was stretched tightly across its arms and seat. It closely resembled pictures of 'the electric chair' I'd seen in a magazine. The base of the contraption was able to swing and had a hydraulic foot pump to raise and lower the victim. Immediately above the chair was a powerful lamp that forced you to keep your eyes tight shut during Mr Price's workmanship. The pain he inflicted on you carrying out these surgical duties produced a similar response.

I was shaking with fear and my eyes hurriedly picked up information about the room and its contents. The sight of the bubbling sterilizer in the corner, the glass shelving and cupboards bearing stainless steel instruments and the cylinders of nitrous oxide anaesthetic gas increased my heart rate even more. I saw a syringe with a needle the size of a harpoon, a mixing dish bearing stale grey amalgam and, to my left, the drill. This contraption looked as though it would be less out of place in a foundry than in a place of medical care. A system of wires locked into pulley mechanisms and steel universal joints gave it a supposed versatility. The terminal component of this machine was the drill-head, about the size of a thick pencil. I had experienced this gadget before when Mr Price had given me a filling and I had been spitting enamel shrapnel for weeks. The drill bit seemed to whir and rotate so slowly that the clumsy gimlet would frequently bounce off the tooth undergoing treatment onto other healthy teeth. Subsequently, due to his lack of dexterity, they too soon developed tooth decay.

It was the mouth gag that really terrified me. This device, made from stainless steel and rubber, was designed to keep your mouth wide open during a filling or an extraction. It was a dreadful feeling as your jaws now stretched wide open almost beyond their limit. Patients would nearly drown in their saliva.

'What's giving you trouble, eh? Open wide,' commanded Mr Price as he took a probe from a glass tray.

'It's this one,' I said pointing to the decaying mass of enamel. 'But it feels ok at the moment,' I continued.

'Ooooh... that'll have to come out, lad,' he said as he stared into my mouth.

'Yes, Mrs Makepeace, we'll have to draw this premolar, lower right second, if you'll make a note of that, please?'

What did he want to draw it for I thought? Maybe he was going to sketch it so he knew what *it looked like for next time? I might be going home without him pulling it after all.*

Well, I certainly did not see any pencil. All that did come into view was that terrifying mouth gag in his nicotine-stained hands and it was heading my way.

'Right, open your mouth wide, and I mean wide, lad,' he instructed. I did as I was told. He pushed the device inside me, through my open lips, and I bit on the rubber-covered bars. It had so much power it was tearing my jaws apart. Out of the corner of my eye I saw Mrs Makepeace approaching me. She had heard me squeal with discomfort and I thought she was coming to console my petrified form. I felt her warm arm on my left shoulder. She touched me like a surrogate mum. Oooh... I mused, that was reassuring, she won't let him hurt me. Then, to my surprise, she quickly slipped that same arm round the base of my neck and locked my head into an immovable position.

'Now relax and you won't feel anything,' she firmly advised.

Mr Price went over to the gas cylinders and picked up a triangular-shaped mask attached to a length of dull, grey concertina tubing. I was gripping the chair so hard that my fingers blanched. My heart was about to burst from my chest as the mask was pushed firmly against my face.

'Now just breathe in and out normally,' he said. Normally? I was just about to have the inside of my mouth ripped apart and he asked me to breathe normally? I was breathing alright but as though I'd just finished the 100 yards race.

It was the feeling of being asphyxiated, together with the stench of the perished parts of the rubber mask, that I found intolerable. The taste of the gas too played havoc with my olfactory senses and made me want to pull the thing off. As I attempted to wriggle and raise my hands to grab the thing, Mrs Makepeace handcuffed both my arms with her remaining free right hand.

'Steady on son! Steady on, it will soon be over,' she grunted down my ear. I could resist no more as the gas started to take its effect.

Anaesthesia in those days was just a couple of steps up from chloroform in a hanky, or getting lashed with rum and biting on a stick. The gas did, however, induce slumber but with appalling side-effects. I distinctly remember, throughout the course of my coma, loud buzzing noises going on and off. I was aware of repeated loud screams followed by wailing noises. Then, paving the way for my reintegration with the conscious world, thumping sounds pounded my ears as my eyes started to open.

'All over now! All done now!' shouted Mrs Makepeace.

'Put his head between his knees for a minute,' instructed Mr Price. 'He looks a bit pale,' he added.

I came out of the anaesthetic very slowly. I felt as though I had been struck by a double-decker bus.

'Rinse yer mouth with this and spit it into here!' Mrs Makepeace advised. I quaffed the pink liquid several times, only to spit a scarlet fluid into the funnel nearby.

Thank God it's over. Never again do I want to endure anything like this. My mouth ached and my head banged incessantly. Mrs Makepeace gave me a rectangular piece of lint and told me that I was to mop up any blood coming from the corner of my mouth, should it bleed a little. Bleed a little? I was conscious of having lost about four pints already. I could taste nothing but the stuff in my mouth.

I climbed out of the chair and observed Mr Price go to the back of the room and open a window. He then lit a roll-up and blew a puff of smoke into the air outside.

'If you get any problems, come back and let me know. You may find a couple of aspirins will help you sleep tonight,' was his parting advice.

I wanted out of this place as quickly as possible and my exit from this room was a mixture of a drugged stagger and a run. Little Albie was the first person I encountered in the waiting room that now contained a few more of Mr Price's patients. I must have looked awful for, indeed, I certainly felt so. Albie's jaw would have dropped if it hadn't been for the scarf round his head. I saw his face go a deathly white and he grabbed for his mother's arm.

'Albie Crump?' called Mrs Makepeace from inside the surgery door.

My exit from the premises was interrupted by a small figure pushing me out of the way. A young lad in urine-soaked short trousers and a knotted scarf on his head was shouting at the top of his voice.

'I ain't goin' in there, mam! Yer can get lost, all er yo! I ain't goin' in!' screamed Albie as he jumped down the steep steps and disappeared in a vapour trail along Broad Street. I never knew he could move so fast.

Well, that was that. I'd had it taken out. Never... never again. I'm going to brush my teeth twenty times a day from now on. Signing the pledge to affirm a commitment to such a change in lifestyle and ablutions was unsurprisingly made easier as I heard a whirring sound starting up inside the surgery as another pour soul became a victim of Mr Price's drill.

One, Two, Cha-Cha-Cha

'You'll thank me for it in the future. Just mark my words!' bellowed my garrulous Auntie Cissie.

'Me and your mother have been discussing it and we both think it's the right thing to do,' she continued.

'Do I have to?' was my anaemic reply.

'Yes, you do. It'll come in handy for weddings, anniversaries and... things. I've sent off for a suit for you from the catalogue an' all. Mind you, that's your Christmas and birthday presents for the next couple of years. Your mother's had a look at your school shoes and she said they'll do.'

My aunt was never short of words, and sentences came out of her mouth like bullets from a Bren gun. This rather unilateral debate focussed on my rights of passage and her *idée fixe* was the need for me to learn ballroom dancing. This skill, according to my aunt, would be the making of me. I would then be able to enjoy myself at these tedious social events and thus allow my relatives to comment on how grown-up I looked whisking my Auntie Minnie around the Pendleton Assembly Rooms dance floor. Her rationale, however, was completely at odds with my fifteen-year-old person and its high levels of testosterone.

It just didn't sound a very masculine thing to do, quickstepping around a polished floor. I was a Salford lad, after all, and me taking part in ballroom dancing was like asking me to compromise my gender. I liked playing rugby league and warmed to a life of bruises, broken noses and spitting teeth. I could never imagine the likes of Salford RLFC's Charlie Bott tripping the light fantastic and then advising his partner about sequins.

Trying to reason with these powerful ladies in my life proved impossible. Cissie's recalcitrant and overbearing personality made her the Papa Doc of Pendleton and so my immediate social calendar was sorted. It was my mother who made the prospect of spending a couple of hours a week prancing around a ballroom sound more appealing.

'Put it this way, love,' she whispered as Cissie marched off into the kitchen, 'you may meet some lovely girls there.'

I hadn't thought of this possibility. I was too concerned with my mates discovering I was about have an impending sex change and 'bat for the other team'. They mustn't find out at all cost. I would gain little cachet in the five-a-side football team warbling on about chasses and spin-turns. Best to keep mum about this newly-prescribed, life-changing venture.

I enrolled at The Court School of Dancing, situated above the Broadway Cinema in the centre of Eccles. I was confident that no-one would know me there since it was a bus ride from Pendleton. The suit Cissie had bought me was brown simulated mohair. It was a perfect fit as long as I stooped forward slightly to eliminate a large diagonal crease in the jacket that stretched from shoulder to vent. If I stood in this semi-kyphosed position, you couldn't tell it was there. The trouble came when I would try to perform the dance steps with a partner. I looked quite creepy as I held them and then suddenly leant forward with my head now over their shoulders.

'Er, do you have to do that? Yer breathing down me ear 'ole!' exclaimed one fellow dance student who found my sudden shift in posture rather disturbing. After some deliberation, I decided to look less pervy and I soon became less conscious of this sartorial blunder.

When I first attended the centre, I paid my money at the kiosk and went upstairs, then through the glass doors into the ballroom. I tried to look casual but, at the same time, work out what I should do. Some of the people there were in their late teens, others in their twenties but the majority looked ancient. Some were well over forty!

I was doing well at being as unobtrusive as possible. There was a soft drinks bar on one side of the room and so, to complete the relaxed air I believed I was successfully creating, I decided to purchase a bottle of something and lean against a pillar. I'd seen Errol Flynn do this in one of his films – very impressive.

The most intoxicating beverage they sold was shandy. For it to have any stimulating effect on your nervous system, you would have to consume around two hundred bottles of the stuff. I pulled out the sixpence given to me by my mother and delivered my request to the lady behind the bar.

'A bottle of shandy, please?' I said in a seasoned way worthy of Ray Milland.

'How old are you? Eh?' came an abrupt response from the lady.

'Er, eighteen,' was my reflex attempt at seniority.

'You can 'ave orange squash and that's all. Eighteen indeed! That's threepence halfpenny,' retorted the bar detective.

I was collecting my change, still trying to remain nonchalant in spite of the reprimand when I suddenly felt a tap on my shoulder. I quickly turned around only to see a lad I knew, Desmond Lomax.

'What are you doin' here?' he inquired.

'Never mind that Dessie, what are you doin' here?' I replied.

'Me big sister Noreen is getting married soon and me mam said I had to learn the waltz for the reception,' he explained.

Dessie had four sisters, no brothers. His dad had cleared off a couple of years ago and was living in Urmston with a packer from the Colgate-Palmolive factory in Trafford Park.

'Yer dad's not back then?' I asked.

'No. No chance. Me mam wouldn't have him back anyway. Well, why are you 'ere?'

'I suppose it's for the same reason as you, Dessie. My mum and Auntie Cissie say I've got to learn to dance for social reasons. Is this your first time here?' I moaned.

'No, I started last week. I'm givin' it three more goes and then if I can't waltz by that time, it's hard luck.'

Dessie then explained to me the course of the evening. The mass of eager Fred Astaire and Ginger Rogers wannabees were split into two ability groups, the intermediates and the absolute beginners. The former lot would learn the complexities of the slow foxtrot and *paso doble*, whilst our clan of virgin dancers would keep to the basics of the waltz and cha-cha. At the end of this hour long tuition, there was a thirty-minute 'excuse me' session when music was played and things were less formal. You could ask ladies for a dance.

The two groups would congregate at different ends of the ballroom. Each bunch was under the supervision of an instructor. Our choreographer was a lady named Eileen Duffy. She was an extremely loud and demonstrative character, and a teacher of PE at the local secondary modern school. My initial thoughts about the lady were that she would not have been out of place teaching Boadicea a few combat moves on an Iceni training course.

Some members of our group had less rhythm than me. One lady, by the name of Beverley, wore silver dancing shoes. She must have polished them before each session because she always smelt of Duraglit. Beverley's feet did not obey the laws of time and were always a few seconds behind everyone else. Consequently a command from the instructor of,

'And one, two, three ...and one, two, three,' Beverley's feet would on each occasion include a four.

Dessie was hardly Victor Sylvester as well. He put his feet down like ready money and his leg movements mimicked the goose-stepping of the Waffen SS. Even the teacher, Mrs Duffy, picked this up. You could tell by the way she cruelly offered him advice,

'Oy, Heinrich Himmler over there!' she would call. 'You're supposed to be dancing with her, not kickin' her to death!'

By the end of week three, I'd had enough. Dessie had completed his compulsory stint and was now equipped to crush the feet of his relatives at any wedding or bar mitzvah. I was seriously tempted to go to the pictures instead of going to The Court. However, I suddenly remembered the interrogation I received when I arrived home. My mother would ask me to show her the steps I'd learned, so unfortunately week four's lesson was on its way.

She entered the ballroom with a friend. She was the most beautiful girl I had ever seen. Her alabaster skin contrasted with her golden curls. She moved serenely across the dance floor and joined the improvers' group. I couldn't take my eyes off her. The clothes she wore looked quality and her make-up had been carefully applied to give her a neat, yet stunning, appearance. I was smitten. I was in love.

I bungled my way through our beginners' session, but all the time my eyes were drawn to this beauty who seemed to glide effortlessly across the floor. At the start of the 'excuse me' I watched a stream of young men ask her to dance. This young lady was out of my league. She passed by me during a quickstep; an impossible dance for me to learn. I noticed her limpid blue eyes and when she smiled this seemed only to intensify her comeliness.

The number 64 bus took me home. I couldn't remember the journey. All I could think of was the girl with the flaxen hair.

'How did you get on, love?' my mother asked as she was halfway through a pile of ironing.

'Oh, pretty well,' I replied. 'Do you know, mum, I think I've quite taken to this dancing lark. Can I have some extra lessons?'

'Well, you're going to have to pay for them yourself, I'm still paying for your bike on the drip,' she stressed.

'That's alright, mum, I'll use that Christmas money I haven't spent. Oh and do you know what happened to that after shave that Auntie Lena bought me?' I queried.

The next week saw me at The Court School of Dancing, smelling of an overpowering lotion whose fragrance was not dissimilar to a cocktail of pear drops and wood preserver. It certainly didn't smell like that in the bottle, it just seemed to change in chemistry when applied to the skin. I would refrain from dousing myself in this salve in future weeks in view of some of the comments I received from my fellow dance tutees.

'Who's been creosoting?' asked one student standing a few metres from me.

'What's that funny smell? Has someone got Athlete's Foot?' inquired another. It was all acutely embarrassing and would certainly not entice my golden-haired beauty — well, not unless she was a fence paneller or a nurse.

Each visit to the dance academy seemed to draw me deeper in love. It was everything about her that ruled my mind. She was so perfect. A sophisticate, if ever I'd seen one. The closest I got to her was once when I was dancing with a corpulent lady with an enormous bosom. This lady's frontage made it difficult for me to put my arms around her waist. It was like dancing with her single—handed and not knowing what to do with the right arm.

I overheard someone call my loved one, Susan. Well, that was it. I now had a name for my beloved.

Over the next weeks my love for Susan intensified. I was eager to impress her and so I borrowed Raymond McCarthy's suede shoes and knitted tie in an attempt to complete the mature image. The trouble was, one of Ray's shoes squeaked quite loudly. Not all of the time, just occasionally. It didn't do my cool image much good and it was like waiting for a bomb to explode. People would look round as well. However, during one really bad session, the shoe went crazy and squeaked incessantly, leading some to believe the place was infested with mice.

I was punched in the eye playing rugby against Burnage Grammar School and I now possessed a large lump over my left eye, with some patchy bruising. This injury complemented the image I wanted to create – tough, macho, interesting and enigmatic. Would she notice my injury? Would she think I was a fearless and talented sportsman? Would she be attracted to my new rugged and androgenic appearance?

It was at the end of week fourteen's lesson that I finally summoned the confidence to ask her to dance. The problem was that me and every other male wanted to do the same thing. I had to find some way of putting the shortest distance between me and the lovely Susan, so that I could reach her before any of the other suitors. My plan was to go into the gents' toilets just before the start of the 'excuse me' session and then to pounce as she returned to her seat. Unfortunately, my first attempts at adopting this strategy failed miserably. Some of the young men with whom I was in competition had more acceleration than Jesse Owens. A worrying factor too was that I was seen to be frequently hanging around the toilets. This didn't do my street cred much good. I gave the appearance of being either a closet homosexual or someone with a chronic urinary problem.

One evening I almost made it. Well, almost. The instructor announced the period of 'excuse me' and I came out of the gents' as though I was about to miss the last bus. I was a couple of yards away from her when, from nowhere, a tall bloke with side-burns and a creamed DA appeared and whisked her away for a waltz. I now had to quickly think what I should do. Why was I walking over here?

Should I do a U-turn? Should I just carry on walking? I must maintain my cultivated cool image and, before I knew anything, I was asking the corpulent lady with the large bosom to dance. We shuffled around the floor to the dulcet tones of Jim Reeves, my right arm being once more redundant. I made a few attempts at lunging for her waist but unfortunately I only managed to put my hands on the side of her left breast. I resigned myself to dancing with one hand in my jacket pocket, in a similar way to the Duke of Edinburgh when he takes a stroll.

The weeks passed and I now became proficient with both the waltz and the cha-cha. Spin turns were out, unfortunately, I just guided my partners around right-angled corners like steering a ship. This worked well as long as I allowed myself enough time to complete the manoeuvre. In my early days of choreographic gallivanting, I admit to sending some of my dance partners into chairs. These navigational mistakes proved extremely humiliating as the noise of the collision made people turn, only to see me apologising profusely to my partner as I helped her from her newly-acquired supine repose.

I suppose I was Walter Mitty. I imagined myself in all sorts of situations and Susan was there with me. She was excited about everything I did. My fantasies included her seeing me score a try or solve difficult physics problems. I would walk alongside her through Peel Park with equanimity, her laughing at my jokes and being impressed by my intelligent remarks and conversation. I would protect her from a savage dog and then take her for afternoon tea at the Alhambra Tea Rooms near

Piccadilly. She was, of course, a class act and deserved only the best. There we would exchange witty banter and peruse The Guardian and check the starting time of Pinter's, 'The Homecoming', at the Library Theatre, which we would watch later that day.

It was a splendid episode of make-believe but nevertheless made me even more determined that our relationship should blossom. I would definitely ask her to dance this evening and, using my urbane charm, a deep and fulfilling relationship would undoubtedly follow.

I changed tactics that evening. I decided to sit at a table some yards from her and, as soon as she had completed a couple of token 'excuse me' dances with the hoi polloi, I would swoop with all the sang froid and composure I could muster. I looked at my watch and there was only five minutes of 'excuse me' time remaining. She had been token dancing non-stop with riff-raff and I was worried my new strategy would mean yet another week of delusion.

The last dance of the evening was announced as a cha-cha and I leapt from my seat as though I had sat on a sea urchin. I went straight for my target, accidentally stepping on the foot of the large-breasted woman who was resting two tables away.

'Good God, lad!' she complained, as she rubbed the trodden foot. 'It's alright, I've got another.'

Following this plantar trauma, my approach to Susan's table was more of a stagger than an insouciant swagger. She turned around to witness me hurtling towards her at forty-five degrees and I clung onto her table to arrest my newly-induced momentum.

'Ruddy hell, kid!' she screamed. 'I thought ya was attackin' me.'

This loud and undignified Salfordian riposte came from my Susan.

Slightly confused by her guttural outburst, I was still determined to ask her to dance as a sweetener before I asked her to share my life forever more.

'Would you like to dance?' I asked, as I let go of the table.

'Oh blimey, I'm knackered, cock,' she said, fanning herself with a beer mat and readjusting the table's position. 'Ask me pal, I'm sweatin.'

I stood there, unable to comprehend what I had just heard. I was stunned by it all. Susan didn't speak like this. She was refined, sophisticated and gentle.

I dropped my head in shock and disappointment. My illusions had been destroyed in a ten second burst. I turned to go back towards the gents' and I started to feel a lump in my throat. I was filling up. I think I was starting to cry. A deep voice then ripped into my melancholy.

'Well, ya can dance wi' me after nearly breaking me leg. That's the least you can do.'

It was the large-bosomed lady, on hand to offer an instant prescription for mending my shattered life.

'One, two, cha-cha-cha. One, two, cha-cha-cha. You know the steps, don't you, love? And cheer up, you look as though you've lost a pound and found sixpence!'

How little she knew.

Lightning Source UK Ltd.
Milton Keynes UK
UKOW052351020212

186552UK00002B/93/P